MW01097846

U.S. Presidents

Author: George Lee
Editor: Mary Dieterich
Proofreaders: Alexis Fey and Margaret Brown

COPYRIGHT © 2020 Mark Twain Media, Inc.

ISBN 978-1-62223-819-4

Printing No. CD-405051

Mark Twain Media, Inc., Publishers
Distributed by Carson-Dellosa Publishing LLC

The purchase of this book entitles the buyer to reproduce the student pages for classroom use only. Other permissions may be obtained by writing Mark Twain Media, Inc., Publishers.

All rights reserved. Printed in the United States of America.

Visit us at www.carsondellosa.com

Table of Contents

To the Teacher

This book profiles the presidents of the United States. Each lesson includes a reading selection with a presidential biography including the person's early years, how they became president, what happened during their term or terms in office, and how they spent their years after leaving office. The Recalling Key Details page features activities focused on using the informational text to develop reading comprehension skills. Enhancement activities are also included for each president at the back of the book. These creative, hands-on activities include suggestions for graphic organizers, discussion questions, creative writing assignments, artistic projects, map analysis, and research opportunities.

Introduction: The Making of a President

The Constitution offers few obstacles to becoming president. It requires only that the person be at least 35 years old, born in the United States or of U.S. citizens, and have spent 14 years in the United States. If those were the only criteria, over 70 million Americans would be eligible to become president. But obviously there are more hurdles that separate a person from the office. The fact that we have had no women, Asian, or Latino presidents in the past does not mean it will never happen. It means only that in the past, they have never been considered for the office. In recent years, an African-American man was elected president and there was a female presidential candidate for the Democratic party. As the makeup of the American people changes, so too does the

leadership of the country, although that change may lag behind the trends of society.

The Constitution requires that the president be chosen by the Electoral College. In the early days of the nation, the electors were chosen by state legislatures, but by the 1830s, the people were choosing the electors. The number of electors a state has is equal to the number of members it is entitled to in the House of Representatives and Senate. Every state has two senators, but the number in the House is based on population. A state with five House members has seven electors (5 + 2), while a state with 20 House members has 22 electors (20 + 2). This has often affected who will be chosen as a presidential candidate. Candidates from states with large numbers of electoral votes have a better chance of being chosen than those from states with small populations.

A candidate must be nominated by a political party. George Washington was the only exception. The parties began to form in the 1790s, and while the party labels have changed over the years, the role of political parties has not. The political parties are groups that form around a leader or a common cause. They first developed from the debate over the Constitution; those favoring it were called Federalists and those opposing it were called Anti-Federalists. Today, the major parties are the Republicans and the Democrats. Besides the major parties, we have had a number of "third" parties that have come along, and in some cases, these parties have affected the national election. In 1912, the third-party candidate, Theodore Roosevelt, received more votes than the Republican candidate, William H. Taft, which may have led to the Democratic candidate, Woodrow Wilson, being elected.

To win the party nomination is very important, but what does it take to do that? A person must have ambition and want the job badly enough to work hard to get it. The campaign process is a torture test of developing policy statements, giving speeches, shaking hands, organizing, raising money, and avoiding costly mistakes. A candidate chosen in the twenty-first century will probably spend at least two years of hard work to get nominated. The candidate has to believe in himself or herself, as well as the policies he or she wants to carry out when they get elected.

The candidate must also be intelligent. He or she must take a position on a wide variety of topics and then defend his or her decisions on foreign and domestic policies. In the past, some candidates were able to get by with vague statements about where they stood on issues, but voters like to know specifics about what the candidate's plans are.

Introduction: The Making of a President (cont.)

Personality certainly makes a difference. A person who is charming, witty, is careful about controlling his or her temper, and chooses words well is going to draw media attention and adoring supporters. However, having a unique and boisterous personality can distinguish a candidate from the rest of the crowd and can win the candidate supporters. The role of personality has become more important in the age of television and the Internet.

Appearance is important. The candidate must look like a leader and act like one. Image is important to success in seeking high office.

The candidate must be able to draw support from a wide variety of backers. The candidate has to be appealing to senior citizens, working moms, the rich, the poor, the middle class, and people from a wide variety of religious, racial, and ethnic backgrounds in order to win. The candidate does not have to please everyone, but he or she has to please enough people to get the support needed for a strong campaign.

The candidate has to have good advisors to help guide him or her in weak areas. A person growing up in New York City may understand city issues but have no knowledge of agricultural issues. He or she may have been a governor and understand how an executive branch works, but be weak in foreign policy. A senator may have experience with the legislative branch and maybe even foreign policy, but he or she will need guidance in administration. Getting the right advice is critical to running for office successfully.

Being decisive is also important. If the candidate cannot make a firm decision and stick to it, the public will wonder if he or she is capable of being a strong leader for the nation. On the other hand, sticking to a policy that draws too much opposition is foolhardy. The candidate has to know when to compromise and when to stand firm.

The same qualities that make a good candidate make a person successful as president: ambition, intelligence, personality, appearance, keeping public support, choosing good advisors, and

being decisive. It also helps to have a family that does not embarrass, a spouse who can turn on the charm, and a good economic situation and world peace during his or her term of office.

This book is about those who have served as president. It will try to describe the individual's background and his successes and failures in the highest office in our land. As future voters of the United States, you will be choosing future presidents. When it is your turn to vote, study the candidates, decide for yourself what qualities you like and dislike in each of them, and choose which will make the nation stronger and better.

GEORGE WASHINGTON
(1732–1799, P. 1789–1797).

When the electors cast their ballots in 1789, they unanimously chose George Washington for president. He was the most famous American of his time and was noted for his courage and character. The old saying goes: "As the twig is bent, so the tree is inclined." He intended for his "tree," the presidency, to stand straight, tall, and proud.

Washington was the son of Augustus and Mary. His father was often away taking care of his iron ore business, so young George was with his mother most of the time. Little schooling was available in the area, and George Washington had only seven or eight years in classrooms. He was best at mathematics. He also learned the social skills required of a person in the upper class. Perhaps the part he enjoyed most was dancing. Much of his time was spent outdoors working, hunting, and fishing. He loved riding horses and exploring the woods. When George was 11 years old, his father died, and he inherited the family farm, along with several enslaved people. George ran the plantation and became an excellent farmer. He was also a surveyor on the Virginia frontier.

George's half-brother, Lawrence, had been a militia captain, and he taught George about military subjects. Lawrence died in 1752 of tuberculosis, and after the death of Lawrence's wife and daughter, George inherited the plantation at Mount Vernon, including more enslaved workers.

In 1753, Washington was made a major in the Virginia militia. He was sent to the frontier to the forks of the Ohio River where the French were building Fort Duquesne (at Pittsburgh) and was involved in one of the early encounters that led to the French and Indian War. Washington was with British General Braddock's failed expedition against the French. He was later assigned the job of protecting Virginia's frontier.

He married Martha Custis in 1759; she was a widow with two children and a large estate. He then served in the colonial legislature. There he learned how difficult it was to get bills passed. He also met many future leaders like Patrick Henry and Thomas Jefferson. He watched as the colonies and England drifted toward war.

In 1775, Congress chose him to lead its army. He refused to take a salary, and Congress only paid for his expenses. "These are times that try men's souls," Thomas Paine wrote, and certainly that was true for Washington. Defeated in battle many times, he refused to quit. He suffered through cold winters with his men, saw men desert, and complained to Congress about their need for shoes and blankets. It has been said that Washington was at his best when conditions were at their worst. He never considered giving up. His efforts paid off in 1781 at Yorktown, Virginia, with a major victory. Great Britain finally gave the United States its independence.

Washington returned to Mount Vernon, expecting to spend the rest of his life as a farmer. However, he left retirement again when the Constitutional Convention was held in 1787. He was elected president of the Convention, and then he was chosen as the first president of the United States in 1789. It was a job he did not want or ask for, but he put public interest before personal desire.

WASHINGTON AS PRESIDENT. Washington faced five important problems. Problem 1 was organizing the executive branch; he did that by choosing a cabinet. At the time, it had only three members: the secretary of state, secretary of the treasury, and secretary of war.

Problem 2 was putting the government on a sound financial basis. That was done by the policies of Secretary of the Treasury Alexander Hamilton. The Bank of the United States was created to handle government funds. When frontier farmers protested against the Whiskey Tax, Washington sent an army to enforce it. When the farmers surrendered, he pardoned them.

Problem 3 was getting the British to leave forts in the West, which was finally accomplished by the Jay Treaty. When wars broke out in Europe between Great Britain and France, Washington stayed neutral. The country was not yet strong enough to get involved in world affairs, and he was able to stay neutral, despite the general opinion that the United States should help France.

Problem 4 was trouble with Native Americans on the frontier. Three expeditions were sent to fight Native Americans. The first two ended in humiliating disasters. The third was led by General Anthony Wayne, and the Native Americans were defeated at Fallen Timbers.

Problem 5 was to create an image for the United States. Remember, at that time, the United States was a very small nation with a weak army and navy. The president was always dignified, holding fancy levees (receptions) and dinners. He said: "There is a rank due to the United States among nations which will be withheld, if not absolutely lost, by the reputation of weakness." He gave every appearance that the United States was in strong hands.

Many issues came up where Washington had to take an unpopular stand, but he always made difficult decisions without concern for personal glory. He knew as much about war and foreign affairs as anyone, so he kept a close eye on the War and State Departments. Economic affairs were more difficult for him to understand, so he gave the secretary of the treasury more freedom to make decisions in that area. He expected honesty and integrity from everyone in government, and would accept nothing less.

After eight years as president, and despite many pleas that he serve another term, he retired and gladly returned to his plantation at Mount Vernon. He voluntarily did what few people with great power had ever done before; he gladly gave up power for a quiet life with his family. His main activity now was raising crops and supervising his workers.

Despite relying on enslaved labor for his entire life, Washington came to believe that the practice of slavery was not good for the nation economically. He thought a gradual abolition of slavery might be best for the country. Although he never used his position to call for abolition, in his will, he arranged for the enslaved people he owned to be freed after the death of his wife. Martha Washington legally freed those enslaved people in 1801, a year before she died.

When Washington died in 1799, the nation mourned its loss. He was praised by Richard Henry Lee as being "First in war, first in peace, and first in the hearts of his countrymen." He had performed well every job he had been given and had fearlessly done what he thought was in the best interests of his people.

Washington has been honored by the nation in many ways. A state, the nation's capital, and many counties, cities, schools, and streets bear his name. The Washington Monument is by far the tallest structure in the District of Columbia, and his face appears on the quarter and the $1 bill.

Name: _____ Date: _____

Recalling Key Details

Directions: Answer the following questions using what you have learned from the reading selection.

True/False:

Write *T* if the statement is true or *F* if it is false.

____ 1. George Washington was highly educated in prestigious schools.

____ 2. Washington began running his family's farm when he was 11.

____ 3. Washington had military experience fighting in France.

____ 4. As the first president, Washington had to set up the Cabinet and portray an image of strength for the office and the nation.

____ 5. Washington publicly spoke out against the institution of slavery.

Multiple Choice:

6. Which of these did not happen while George Washington was a young man?

    A. His father and brother died   B. He inherited land and several enslaved people

    C. He became a surveyor   D. He became a sailor

7. Which of these was not one of the problems of Washington's presidency?

    A. Getting the British to leave frontier forts   B. Dealing with Native Americans

    C. Building a new national capital   D. Establishing a sound financial base

Structured Response:

8. Washington is not as popular now as he was a century ago. Why do you think that is?

_____

_____

_____

9. What qualities might a general have that would be helpful as president? _____

_____

_____

10. What qualities might a general have that would hurt them as president? _____

_____

_____

JOHN ADAMS
(1735–1826, P. 1797–1801)

Washington, D.C., was a city in name only when John Adams moved into the Executive Mansion in 1800. There were tree stumps where roads were to be built and a swamp down by the Potomac River.

Adams was born in Braintree (now Quincy), Massachusetts, in 1735. His family was of old Puritan stock and had come to America around 1640. Young Adams worked on the family farm and studied in the village school. He graduated from Harvard College in 1755, became a teacher while he studied law, and became a lawyer in 1758.

Adams married Abigail Smith in 1764. She was an intelligent woman who was poorly educated, but she became a good reader, learned French, and was a writer of interesting letters. She was one of John's closest advisors and managed the family home and farm when John was away for work. They had six children, two who died in infancy. She joined her husband in Paris and London when he was a diplomat there.

Adams opposed the Stamp Act in 1765 on the basis the colonies were not represented in Parliament. In 1768, he moved to Boston, where his cousin, Sam Adams, was stirring up the people against the British in creative ways. John and Sam did not always think alike, however. When British soldiers were tried for the Boston Massacre, John defended them in court.

Adams was a member of the Continental Congress, and he strongly argued for independence. He was a member of the committee appointed to write a Declaration of Independence; Thomas Jefferson wrote the famous document, but Adams defended it when Congress debated it. He served in France and Holland as a diplomat during the Revolution. At the end of the Revolution, he was sent to Paris to negotiate peace terms with Great Britain. In 1785, he was appointed as American ambassador to Great Britain.

In 1789, Adams was chosen as vice president by the electors. He called the vice presidency "the most insignificant office that ever the invention of man contrived or his imagination conceived."

In 1796, Adams was elected president, and Thomas Jefferson was elected vice president. By this time, the two men were no longer friends. Jefferson suspected that Adams favored monarchy and disliked him personally. Adams was a hard person to like; he was vain, opinionated, bad-tempered, and stubborn.

ADAMS AS PRESIDENT. When the United States and France were close to fighting a war in 1798, Federalists in Congress passed the Alien and Sedition Acts, making it a crime for anyone to criticize the president or Congress. There was a storm of protest against the new laws; Jefferson and James Madison secretly wrote resolutions passed by the Kentucky and Virginia legislatures attacking the Sedition Act as a violation of the First Amendment. The laws were clearly a legal and political blunder. The possible war with France cleared when Adams defied Federalist opinion and sent a delegation to France to settle differences. He had lost Republican support over the Sedition Act, and then he lost Federalist support over the negotiations with France.

When Jefferson was elected to replace him, Adams refused to stay for the inauguration. He left office a lonely and bitter man. However, in his old age, he renewed his friendship with Jefferson. As he lay dying on July 4, 1826, 50 years to the day after the Declaration of Independence, his last words were "Thomas Jefferson still survives." He did not know that Jefferson had died that same morning.

Name: _____ Date: _____

Recalling Key Details

Directions: Answer the following questions using what you have learned from the reading selection.

Matching:

____ 1. One employed to conduct negotiations between nations
____ 2. Inciting resistance to or insurrection against those in lawful authority
____ 3. A formal expression of opinion voted by an official body
____ 4. A person owing allegiance to another country; a noncitizen
____ 5. One of a group of religious separatists who had left England and founded the Massachusetts Bay Colony

A. alien
B. diplomat
C. Puritan
D. sedition
E. resolution

Multiple Choice:

6. In which country did John Adams not serve as a diplomat?
   A. Great Britain   B. France
   C. Holland   D. Russia

7. One of the major issues during John Adams' presidency was negotiating with this country to avoid a war.
   A. Great Britain   B. France
   C. Spain   D. Russia

8. Which of these parts of the First Amendment did the Sedition Act probably violate?
   A. Freedom of religion   B. Freedom of speech
   C. Freedom of the press   D. Freedom to peaceably assemble

Structured Response:

9. How did the situation with France cost Adams support from both political parties?

   _____

   _____

   _____

10. Today the vice president is kept busy with public appearances, work on committees, and other duties assigned by the president. What were the official duties of the vice president during John Adams' time?

   _____

   _____

THOMAS JEFFERSON
(1743–1826, P. 1801–1809)

Thomas Jefferson was the son of Peter and Jane Jefferson. From his father Thomas learned to read and write and how to keep farm records. He became an excellent violinist and loved music. His father died when he was 14 years old, and Jefferson had to run a 2,500-acre farm. There were 30 enslaved persons on the plantation who did most of the hard work, however.

When he was 16, Jefferson went to Williamsburg, Virginia's capital, to attend William and Mary College. After graduating, Jefferson became a lawyer. When his law practice became successful, Jefferson built his mansion and named it Monticello; he designed the house and gardens.

In 1772, he married Martha Skelton, a beautiful widow. Shortly after they married, her father died; her share of her father's estate was 11,000 acres and 135 enslaved persons. Only two of the Jeffersons' six children lived to be adults. Martha had poor health throughout their marriage, and she died in 1782.

Like others of his class, Jefferson became involved in his community and his colony's affairs. He was elected to the House of Burgesses (lower house of the Virginia legislature) in 1769. He became well known for his ability to express complex ideas in simple English.

As a delegate to the Second Continental Congress, he was named to the committee that wrote the Declaration of Independence. It is the most outstanding statement of human rights ever written. Jefferson was the main author of the document that says there are certain rights such as "life, liberty and the pursuit of happiness" that cannot be taken away by a ruler. The government's job is to protect those rights, and if it does not, the people have the duty to rebel and to form a new government.

Jefferson also worked for a separation of church and state, arguing that citizens should not be forced to attend church or pay taxes to support a particular church. He considered his Act for Establishing Religious Freedom one of the greatest achievements of his life.

From 1784 to 1789, he represented the United States in France. When he saw the wealth of the French court and the poverty of the people, he understood the emotions behind the French Revolution. He became U.S. secretary of state in 1789 and was the most pro-French member of Washington's administration. Jefferson tired of the attacks on him by the Federalist newspapers, so he resigned from the cabinet in 1793.

In 1796, John Adams, a Federalist, was elected president, and Jefferson, a Democratic-Republican who received the second-most votes, became vice president. After the Alien and Sedition Acts passed, Jefferson secretly wrote the Kentucky Resolution attacking them. Now, he and Adams were political enemies, each trying to win the presidency in 1800. In the election that year, Jefferson and his running mate, Aaron Burr, received the same number of electoral votes (73), because under the original Constitution, electors cast votes for president and vice president on the same ballot, and did not separate their choices for each office. That was corrected by the Twelfth Amendment. The House finally chose Jefferson for president on the thirty-sixth ballot.

JEFFERSON AS PRESIDENT. Jefferson said he preferred "a government rigorously frugal and simple," and he planned to pay off the national debt. He favored cutting the size of the army and navy; he wanted the navy only to patrol along the coastline and feared a standing army as dangerous to liberty. To calm fears he was going to get revenge on the Federalists, he said, "We are all Republicans, we are all Federalists."

One by one, his ideas were tossed aside. For example, when pirates started attacking American ships in the Mediterranean, he sent the navy and marines to punish their ruler at Tripoli.

The rise of Napoleon in France caused great fear among westerners, since France owned the region west of the Mississippi River. Jefferson sent James Monroe to join Robert Livingston, the ambassador in France, to see if the French were willing to sell New Orleans. Instead, they were told Napoleon was willing to sell all of Louisiana to the United States. The area included nearly all of the region from the west bank of the Mississippi River to the crest of the Rocky Mountains, an area equal in size to that east of the Mississippi River. The cost would be $15 million. Monroe and Livingston went far beyond what they had been told to do when they quickly signed the agreement in 1803; it was too good to pass up.

Jefferson thought it was an excellent deal, but he worried about whether the Constitution allowed it. Most Federalists opposed buying this vast area because the people who settled there were likely to be Republicans. Some New Englanders even talked about seceding (leaving) the Union. Good sense prevailed, however, and the Louisiana Purchase was approved, adding 830,000 square miles to the United States.

Most of the region beyond the Mississippi River had never been explored and was unmapped. This led to the Lewis and Clark expedition. Jefferson appointed his personal secretary Meriwether Lewis to lead the Corps of Discovery into the region. Lewis chose William Clark to be his co-leader for the trip. Their journey from 1804 to 1806 took them up the Missouri River and down the Snake and Columbia Rivers to the Pacific Coast. They mapped the region and reported their observations of animal and plant life, the course of rivers, Native Americans, and the weather. Their trip proved that it was possible to travel overland to the Pacific Coast.

Zebulon Pike was also sent to explore the west, but he was captured by the Spanish when he wandered into their territory. He was held as a prisoner in Santa Fe for months but was finally allowed to leave in 1807.

Jefferson disliked Vice President Aaron Burr, as did many others, including Alexander Hamilton. Jefferson was not going to keep Burr as vice president so Burr decided to run for governor of New York. Hamilton wrote a number of letters criticizing Burr's lack of morals and integrity. Burr challenged Hamilton to a duel in 1804, in which he killed Hamilton. Burr went into hiding after that and began planning an expedition into the west. His exact purpose for taking an expedition down the Ohio and Mississippi Rivers isn't known, but it was suspected that he was trying to take land from the United States or Spain. He was arrested and taken to Richmond, Virginia, where he was tried before Chief Justice John Marshall. Jefferson made a great effort to get him convicted, but in the Constitution, the definition of treason is so narrow that he escaped being punished.

Also during this time, the Supreme Court under the leadership of John Marshall began to expand its power. The Supreme Court had little power until it claimed the right to declare an act of Congress unconstitutional in the case of *Marbury v. Madison* in 1803.

Jefferson rejoiced when he retired and was "free to say and do what I please." He sometimes entertained 70 guests in his home at a time, although he was in poor financial shape when he died. He left his mark on the world as a thinker, shaper, and observer of America's growth from colonies into a nation extending two-thirds of the way across the continent. He died on July 4, 1826, the same day as John Adams.

Name: _____ Date: _____

Recalling Key Details

Directions: Answer the following questions using what you have learned from the reading selection.

Matching:

____ 1. A member of the electoral college authorized to vote for president

____ 2. Lower house of the colonial Virginia legislature

____ 3. The action or system of casting a secret vote

____ 4. Leaving the union

____ 5. A journey undertaken for a specific purpose

A. ballot

B. House of Burgesses

C. expedition

D. elector

E. seceding

Multiple Choice:

6. Thomas Jefferson is most well known for writing what document?

  A. The Constitution

  B. The Bill of Rights

  C. The Declaration of Independence

  D. The Act for Establishing Religious Freedom

7. The major land purchase during Jefferson's presidency is known as what?

  A. The Gadsden Purchase

  B. The Louisiana Purchase

  C. The Oklahoma Land Rush

  D. The Florida Buy Back

8. Jefferson disliked this vice president who later shot a man and was tried for treason.

  A. John Adams

  B. John Marshall

  C. Alexander Hamilton

  D. Aaron Burr

Structured Response:

9. How did the powers of the Supreme Court expand under Chief Justice John Marshall?

_____

_____

_____

10. Jefferson was a lawyer and plantation owner with plenty to do. Why do you think he devoted so much time in service to his colony, state, and country?

_____

_____

_____

_____

JAMES MADISON
(1751–1836, P. 1809–1817)

Born into a wealthy Virginia planter's family, James Madison was a sickly child. His childhood playmates were the children of the family's enslaved workers. He was educated by tutors and then attended Princeton University, graduating in 1771 after two years of study.

Too sickly to be a soldier in the Revolution, he played a minor role in the Virginia convention that called for independence and produced the Virginia Declaration of Rights. He served in the Continental Congress as its youngest delegate in 1781. In debate, Madison lost the shyness and self-consciousness he often felt on other occasions.

As a delegate to the Constitutional Convention in 1787, Madison's note-taking and his role in debates and compromises were so important he was later referred to as the "Father of the Constitution." He was also instrumental in getting the Constitution ratified as one of the authors of the *Federalist Papers,* which helped to explain the Constitution to the people. He promised protections for individual freedom would be added by amendment, and as a member of the House, he proposed the amendments we know as the Bill of Rights. They were ratified by the states in 1789.

In 1794, he met Dolley Todd, a young widow, and the two were married three months after they met. Dolley had a son with her first husband, but the Madisons had no children together. The Madison home became a center of social activity, with Dolley as a colorful, lively hostess. An invitation to their home was highly prized.

In 1801, Thomas Jefferson chose Madison as secretary of state. The main issue at this time was that Great Britain blockaded the coastline of Europe, and France began seizing ships. American sailors were being taken from ships and impressed (forced to serve) on British ships.

MADISON AS PRESIDENT. Madison easily won the presidential election of 1808. Americans were angry with the restrictions put on shipping by the British and their interference with American expansion on the frontier. They were suspicious that the British were helping the Native Americans, who were threatening the frontier. Madison did not want to go to war with the British, but when the "War Hawks" faction, led by Speaker of the House Henry Clay, took over Congress in 1811 and public pressure demanded it, he gave in. Now called the War of 1812, New Englanders bitterly opposed what they called "Mr. Madison's War."

Despite the United States not being prepared for war, there were some successes. British fleets were defeated on Lake Erie and Lake Champlain. At the Battle of the Thames and at Horseshoe Bend, Native American forces were defeated.

However, in 1814, a British fleet landed troops near Washington, D.C., and they burned the president's home, the Capitol building, and the Library of Congress. Dolley Madison was able to save some important papers and a portrait of Washington before fleeing the Executive Mansion.

The Treaty of Ghent ended the war in December 1814 with no winners or losers, but the news did not reach the United States before General Andrew Jackson's forces were able to soundly defeat a British force that attacked at New Orleans. It made Americans more proud of their country than ever. Madison's popularity had never been higher.

In 1817, Madison retired to his home, Montpelier, in Virginia and spent the rest of his life as a gentleman farmer and rector of the University of Virginia. He advised President Monroe on foreign policy issues. He also promoted the idea of sending freed slaves to the African colony of Liberia. He died in 1836. After his death, Dolley returned to Washington, D.C., where she died in 1849.

Name: _____ Date: _____

Recalling Key Details

Directions: Answer the following questions using what you have learned from the reading selection.

Matching:

____ 1. First ten amendments to the Constitution that protect
individual rights

____ 2. What New Englanders called the War of 1812

____ 3. Those in Congress who wanted to go to war with
Great Britain

____ 4. Colony in Africa where freed slaves could live

____ 5. Articles that helped explain the Constitution

A. Mr. Madison's War

B. Liberia

C. Bill of Rights

D. *Federalist Papers*

E. War Hawks

Multiple Choice:

6. James Madison is most well known for his role in
   A. The Revolutionary War.
   B. The Constitutional Convention.
   C. The Declaration of Independence.
   D. The Treaty of Ghent.

7. Which of these were victories for the Americans during the War of 1812?
   A. Lake Erie
   B. Washington, D.C.
   C. Battle of the Thames
   D. New Orleans

8. Which of these was not a reason Americans wanted to go to war with Great Britain in 1812?
   A. High taxes on tea and other goods
   B. A naval blockade of the European coastline
   C. Impressing American sailors
   D. Interference on the American frontier

Structured Response:

9. How did Dolley Madison help James' career in politics?

_____

_____

_____

10. What are some of the ways James Madison helped to create and ratify the Constitution?

_____

_____

_____

_____

JAMES MONROE
(1758–1831, P. 1817–1825)

Like most of the previous presidents, James Monroe was a Virginian. He was educated at home at first, then walked several miles to a nearby school. In 1774, he went to Williamsburg to study at William and Mary College, but the students soon formed militia units, and he was made a lieutenant in a Virginia regiment. Monroe's regiment supported Washington's army and he was wounded at the Battle of Trenton. He later became close friends with the Frenchman Lafayette. Monroe eventually achieved the rank of colonel. When fighting died down, he returned to Virginia and studied law under Thomas Jefferson. They became friends for life. Monroe and his wife Elizabeth had three children, one son who died in infancy and two daughters.

Monroe was elected to the Virginia legislature, served in the Confederation Congress, and started a law practice. In 1790, he was chosen for the U.S. Senate. He was minister (ambassador) to France during George Washington's administration. From 1799 to 1802, Monroe was governor of Virginia. From 1803 to 1807, he was sent overseas on diplomatic missions, negotiating the Louisiana Purchase, trying to acquire Florida from Spain, and trying to get Great Britain to stop impressing (seizing) American sailors. He served again in the Virginia legislature and as governor. President Madison chose Monroe to be secretary of state from 1811 to 1817. This was during the War of 1812 with Great Britain, and for part of this time, Monroe was also the secretary of war.

Monroe's victory in the presidential election of 1816 was one of the easiest ever. The Democratic-Republicans were the only political party with any power. Only three states cast votes for the Federalist candidate. The "Era of Good Feeling" had begun. In 1820, only one elector did not vote for Monroe, saying that only Washington deserved to be elected unanimously. The good feelings lasted for about six years.

MONROE AS PRESIDENT. The United States was growing rapidly during Monroe's presidency. In 1817, the U.S. and Great Britain agreed to take their navies off the Great Lakes. In 1818, the majority of the U.S.-Canada boundary was settled at the forty-ninth parallel. The U.S. also acquired Spanish Florida, which at that time extended from the Atlantic Ocean along a narrow strip reaching Baton Rouge, Louisiana. After Americans captured some territory in 1810 and 1813 and General Andrew Jackson's forces took over most of Florida in 1818, the Spanish signed a treaty giving the United States all of Florida.

Monroe and Secretary of State John Quincy Adams worried that Russians moving down from Alaska and European nations seeking to put down revolutions in Latin America would expand their influence in the Western Hemisphere. In 1823's State of the Union message to Congress, Monroe stated what came to be known as the Monroe Doctrine. It warned Europe not to expand or acquire colonies in North or South America. It also said the United States was not going to get involved in European problems.

In 1820, the Missouri Compromise allowed Missouri to enter the Union as a slave state, while Maine entered as a free state. Slavery would be forbidden in the Louisiana Purchase territories north of the 36°30' line of latitude. This only postponed a final settlement of the question of slavery.

The Monroes did not entertain in a grand style. Elizabeth Monroe was not in good health and was a quiet, reserved person. When they did entertain, they often invited secretaries, farmers, ministers, bookkeepers, and merchants.

When Monroe left office, he was as popular as ever; however, the party was splitting apart as rivals rushed to replace him. This led to the brutal struggle for the presidency in 1824.

Name: _____ Date: _____

Recalling Key Details

Directions: Answer the following questions using what you have learned from the reading selection.

Matching:

____ 1. An ambassador to a foreign country
____ 2. A civilian military force that supports the regular army
____ 3. Seizing sailors to force them to serve on another country's ships
____ 4. The majority of the U.S.-Canada border was set at this latitude.
____ 5. Slavery was forbidden in the Louisiana Purchase territories north of this latitude by the Missouri Compromise.

A. 36°30′ N latitude
B. 49° N latitude
C. militia
D. minister
E. impressing

Multiple Choice:

6. What was the highest rank James Monroe achieved in the Virginia militia?
   A. General
   B. Major
   C. Lieutenant
   D. Colonel

7. What office did Monroe never hold?
   A. Speaker of the House
   B. U.S. Senator
   C. Governor of Virginia
   D. Secretary of State

8. Which policy warned European nations to avoid expanding their influence in the Western Hemisphere?
   A. The Missouri Compromise
   B. The Monroe Doctrine
   C. The Treaty of Ghent
   D. The Era of Good Feeling

Structured Response:

9. Why was the time period during Monroe's presidency called "the Era of Good Feeling"?

_____

_____

_____

10. How did the Missouri Compromise deal with the issue of slavery?

_____

_____

_____

_____

JOHN QUINCY ADAMS
(1767–1848, P. 1825–1829)

John Quincy Adams was the oldest son of President John Adams. While Quincy (as he was often called) was growing up, his father was away serving in the Continental Congress. At age 11, he traveled with his father to Europe and attended schools in Paris, Amsterdam, and Leyden. At age 14, he became a private secretary to the American minister to Russia and then was his father's private secretary. In 1785, he returned to the United States to study at Harvard College. He graduated in 1787, read law for three years, and became a lawyer.

From 1794 to 1801, Adams was away from the United States serving as minister to Holland, Portugal, Prussia, and Sweden. He served in the U.S. Senate from 1803 to 1808, and then as minister to Russia (1809–1814) and Great Britain (1815–1817). After that, he did an outstanding job as Monroe's secretary of state, handling of the Florida situation and the Monroe Doctrine.

Adams met Louisa Johnson, an American raised in London, and they married in 1797. They both had strong personalities, and it was not a happy marriage early on. She was often sad and lonely and resented his being away so often. John also suffered from bouts of depression. The couple had five children, three who lived to adulthood. As the president's wife, however, Louisa was an excellent hostess. In their later years, they found happiness working in the anti-slavery and women's rights movements together.

In the election of 1824, the field eventually narrowed from 17 down to four men as the top candidates: Andrew Jackson, the war hero from Tennessee; Adams, the secretary of state; William H. Crawford, the secretary of the treasury; and Henry Clay, the Speaker of the house. When the election took place, the electoral vote was Jackson (99), Adams (84), Crawford (41), and Clay (37). The Twelfth Amendment says if no candidate for president has a clear majority, the House must choose from the top three. The struggle now was between Jackson and Adams. Crawford had suffered a stroke, and Clay threw his support behind Adams after they held a secret meeting. Adams won, but many Americans believed Jackson should have won.

JOHN QUINCY ADAMS AS PRESIDENT. Trouble for the new president began when he appointed Henry Clay as his secretary of state. Jackson and his followers were convinced a secret deal had been made. There were more anti-Adams members in Congress than pro-Adams. Adams tried to rise above politics, but even his vice president and many cabinet members worked against him.

Adams had many projects in mind, but his opponents, who labeled themselves the "Opposition," made fun of them. Adams' ideas included building astronomical observatories, creating a department of the interior and a national university, having the federal government pay for internal improvements (roads and canals), and treating the Creek Indians in Georgia fairly instead of driving them out. He wasn't able to get any of these projects approved.

A high tariff did pass in Congress in 1828 with help from the Northeast. The South opposed it, and the split between North and South caused resentment that would bring on a future crisis.

In the election of 1828, the public supported General Andrew Jackson and elected Jackson as president by a vote of 178 to 83 electoral votes. A bitter John Quincy Adams left town in the morning before Jackson's noon inauguration.

In 1831, Adams was elected to the House of Representatives from a Massachusetts district and served there until 1848. He died shortly after suffering a cerebral hemorrhage while debating an issue in the House.

Name: _____ Date: _____

Recalling Key Details

Directions: Answer the following questions using what you have learned from the reading selection.

Fact/Opinion:

Write *F* if the statement is a fact or *O* if it is an opinion.

_____ 1. John Quincy Adams had opportunities to travel that most young men did not.

_____ 2. Adams' travel led to trouble in his marriage.

_____ 3. Adams should have stayed at home and focused on his law career more.

_____ 4. Adams was the best secretary of state the country had had up to that point.

_____ 5. Many of Adams' ideas would have been good for the country.

Multiple Choice:

6. To which country did John Quincy Adams not serve as minister?
   A. Russia   B. Holland
   C. Portugal   D. Spain

7. Which of Adams' ideas would later become a reality?
   A. Astronomical observatories   B. Department of the interior
   C. A national university   D. Roads built with federal money

8. Who had the most electoral votes in the presidential election of 1824?
   A. John Quincy Adams   B. Andrew Jackson
   C. Henry Clay   D. William H. Crawford

Structured Response:

9. Why did people feel some sort of secret deal had been made between John Quincy Adams and Henry Clay?

   _____

   _____

   _____

10. What were the unique advantages of Adams' early career as a diplomat that should have helped him be an effective president?

   _____

   _____

   _____

   _____

ANDREW JACKSON
(1767–1845, P. 1829–1837)

Andrew Jackson was the third son of poor immigrants from Northern Ireland, and he was the first president born in a log cabin. His father died before he was born, and his mother died when he was 14. At the age of 13, Andrew had joined the militia during the Revolutionary War and served as a messenger. His two brothers died during the war. Andrew was captured and received a scar on his face and hand when a British officer struck him with his sword.

Jackson became wild and reckless, wasting money that he had inherited from his grandfather. He was intelligent, however, and passed the bar exam, becoming a lawyer at age 20. He was appointed as solicitor (prosecuting attorney) in Nashville, Tennessee. There he met and fell in love with Mrs. Rachel Robards. Her army captain husband was rarely at home, they quarreled, and he eventually filed for divorce. Thinking the divorce had been granted, Jackson married Rachel in 1791. However, they found out in December 1793 that the divorce had only become official in September of that year, so they remarried in January 1794. The couple had no children of their own, but they adopted three children and were guardians to eight others.

By buying and selling land, Jackson made a small fortune. In 1796, he bought the Hermitage, a plantation a few miles from Nashville. He also went into politics, serving in the state constitutional convention, the U.S. House in 1796, and the Senate in 1797. He was elected to the state supreme court and served on it for six years.

Jackson's reputation for dueling was first made in 1806 when he shot and killed a man, despite having been shot in the chest himself. There were more duels to follow.

A major general of the Tennessee militia since 1802, Jackson was eager for a fight when the War of 1812 came. He earned his nickname "Old Hickory" when one of his men commented that Jackson was as tough as hickory after marching through 500 miles of rough land so a sick soldier could ride on his horse. Jackson became famous for his victory over the Creek Indians (British allies) at Horseshoe Bend. After allowing women and children to leave, he attacked, killing 800 men. In January 1815, two weeks after the peace treaty to end the War of 1812 was signed, Jackson, along with his army of frontiersmen, pirates, and shop clerks, defeated a well-trained British army at the Battle of New Orleans.

In 1817, Jackson was ordered to stop Native American attacks in Spanish Florida. His army created an international squabble when he executed two British subjects for encouraging Native American attacks, and he took control of all Florida except St. Augustine. Many easterners were not pleased, but westerners applauded his success, and he became their hero.

Jackson almost won the election of 1824, losing to John Quincy Adams only after the House of Representatives had to decide the election. Many people thought he had been cheated out of the presidency.

In 1828, Jackson was eager to run again. The campaign was the most malicious the nation had ever seen. Among charges against Jackson were that he was a murderer, bigamist, slave trader, drunkard, and thief, but it was the attacks on his wife that hurt Jackson the most. When Rachel died in December, he blamed it on Adams and Henry Clay. Since all but two states chose electors by popular vote now, the election was a good test of public opinion. Jackson received 647,000 votes to Adams' 508,000. The electoral vote was more one-sided, 178–83.

JACKSON AS PRESIDENT. A large rowdy crowd showed up for the inaugural address and the reception at the White House. No preparation had been made for the large numbers packing the rooms. Dishes, glasses, and furniture were destroyed, and to avoid being injured in the crush, Jackson climbed out a window and spent the day at a boardinghouse nearby.

While Jackson had an official cabinet to run the executive departments, he usually listened to an informal group of friends that were known as the "Kitchen Cabinet." They were too clever to tell him what he "must" do, but they definitely influenced his thinking. Only Secretary of State Martin Van Buren was an important voice from the real cabinet.

Among the major events of his administration, four will be briefly discussed here.

1. The spoils system. From the old expression, "to the victor belong the spoils" came the nickname "the spoils system" for the practice of replacing people from the old administration with followers of the new president. Some of these people worked hard, but many were unqualified or lazy. While it seemed that every Adams appointee was fired, it was only 10 to 20 percent who were dismissed.

2. The nullification issue. The southern states began to use nullification to prevent the northern states from passing laws that harmed the South. They believed that if Congress passed a law a state did not like, the state could "nullify" it and keep it from being enforced inside its borders. If the federal government tried to enforce the law, the state would secede (leave) from the Union. Jackson finally made his position known in 1830 when he gave a toast, saying: "Our Union, it must be preserved." Calhoun feebly gave the next toast: "The Union, next to our liberty, most dear."

In 1832, South Carolina tried to declare the act raising tariffs (taxes on imports) unconstitutional and threatened to secede if the government tried to collect these new tariffs in their state. Jackson sent troops and naval ships to collect the taxes. Robert Hayne resigned his Senate seat to become governor of South Carolina, and Calhoun resigned as vice president to become the senator from South Carolina. Senator Henry Clay proposed that the tariff be cut as a compromise, and South Carolina withdrew the nullification of the tariff.

3. The election of 1832 and the Bank issue. The election of 1832 was the first where a national convention was used to choose candidates. The National Republicans chose Clay for president, and the Democratic-Republicans chose Jackson for president and Van Buren for vice president. The big issue of the campaign was whether to re-charter the Second Bank of the United States. The Bank was very powerful. Small banks in the West did not like limits on lending, and those wanting to borrow were angry when they could not get a loan. However, the Bank gave money to those running for office to use in their campaigns so many in the House and Senate did not want the Bank to go out of business. In 1832, Clay and Senator Daniel Webster proposed a bill that would re-charter the Bank, even though the charter would not run out for four more years. They hoped it would split the pro-Jackson forces and make it possible for Clay to be elected. Jackson vetoed the bill, and when he won the election, he began taking government money out of the Bank and putting it into state banks.

4. Removal of Native Americans. Jackson did not like Native Americans, and did not want them on valuable farm or mining land in the east. Congress gave him the power to trade land west of the Mississippi River for land in the east, and unfair treaties were forced on Native Americans to get them to move. They suffered greatly during this process. The Cherokees called the trip the "Trail of Tears" because so many died. The Seminoles moved deeper into the Everglades of Florida and fought many years before most finally gave up. The eastern Native Americans were settled in Indian Territory (now Oklahoma).

After his two terms ended in 1837, Jackson moved back to his home at the Hermitage. Andrew Jackson had opened the door of politics for others who came from poor families, and the common people finally felt they had a voice in government.

Name: _____ Date: _____

Recalling Key Details

Directions: Answer the following questions using what you have learned from the reading selection.

Matching:

____ 1. Someone married to two people at the same time

____ 2. Appointing one's followers to political or bureaucratic offices

____ 3. Declaring a law unconstitutional and refusing to abide by it

____ 4. Taxes on imports

____ 5. The journey from the East to Indian Territory where many Cherokee died

A. tariffs

B. bigamist

C. Trail of Tears

D. spoils system

E. nullification

Multiple Choice:

6. Andrew Jackson had a hot temper, especially when it concerned his wife. During what activity did he kill a man?

   A. A court case

   C. A duel

   B. A presidential campaign

   D. A Revolutionary War battle

7. Which of these was not one of Jackson's military victories?

   A. Battle of the Thames

   C. Horseshoe Bend

   B. Battle of New Orleans

   D. Controlling Spanish Florida

8. Who wanted the Second Bank of the United States to be rechartered?

   A. Western banks

   C. Andrew Jackson

   B. Those wanting loans

   D. Senators and representatives

Structured Response:

9. What happened to Mrs. Jackson in the campaign of 1828 that caused Jackson to hate his opponents?

   _____

   _____

   _____

10. If states could nullify acts of Congress, what would happen to the federal government's power?

   _____

   _____

   _____

   _____

MARTIN VAN BUREN
(1782–1862, P. 1837–1841)

Martin Van Buren was born in 1782 in Kinderhook, New York. His family was of Dutch descent and his father owned a small farm and a tavern. The family also owned enslaved workers. After a few years of schooling, Martin moved to New York where he studied law. "Little Van," as he was known (he was only 5'6" tall), became a lawyer in 1803.

Martin married Hannah Hoes in 1807, and the couple had five sons, four of whom lived to adulthood. Hannah died in 1819, and Van Buren never remarried.

In 1812, Van Buren was elected to the New York senate where he supported construction of the Erie Canal. Van Buren was one of the first politicians to use the press to get his party's message out. In 1821, he was chosen for the U.S. Senate. Through the Democratic-Republican party's organization, the Albany Regency, Van Buren continued to control New York politics for many years. The Regency rewarded friends with jobs and punished those who did not obey its policies.

Van Buren organized the opposition to President John Q. Adams. In 1828, he was elected governor of New York, but when Andrew Jackson was elected president, he appointed Van Buren as secretary of state. Since foreign governments were alarmed that a man of Jackson's background could be president, it was up to Van Buren, with his good manners and polished appearance, to calm their fears. However, Van Buren spent most of his time flattering Jackson so he would be chosen as the vice-presidential candidate in 1832.

In 1836, the Democrats (as the Democratic-Republicans were now known) chose Van Buren as their candidate for president. The Whigs ran three candidates against him, but Van Buren, nicknamed "Old Kinderhook," defeated his closest competitor William Henry Harrison 170–73 in electoral votes.

VAN BUREN AS PRESIDENT. At the beginning of his presidency, Van Buren was most concerned that the growth of abolitionism would split North from South. Van Buren said Congress should not interfere with slavery in the states or the District of Columbia.

Soon after Van Buren took office, the economy collapsed. Factories closed, unemployment was high, and farmers lost their land because of unpaid debts. The Panic of 1837 was the result of an economy expanding too quickly, with people borrowing money too freely. States were borrowing money to build railroads and canals. Without the Second Bank of the United States to stop over-lending, the country was in crisis. Van Buren seemed only to be concerned for the welfare of the government, not the individuals who were suffering. He proposed an independent treasury where federal money could be deposited.

The Whigs (the Democrats' opposition), led by Henry Clay and Daniel Webster, said the government should work to save the economy. The financial crisis eased somewhat in 1838, but the weak economy badly hurt Van Buren's chances of reelection in 1840. This time William Henry Harrison won the election 234–60.

Van Buren returned to Kinderhook, where he kept his hand in New York politics. He tried to win the Democratic nomination again in 1844. By this time, he supported the anti-slavery movement, opposing the annexation of Texas as a slave state, so the South would not support him. He also had an unsuccessful run for president on the Free Soil ticket in 1848. He died in 1862.

Name: _____ Date: _____

Recalling Key Details

Directions: Answer the following questions using what you have learned from the reading selection.

True/False:

Write *T* if the statement is true or *F* if it is false.

____ 1. Martin Van Buren was from a German family.

____ 2. Van Buren's family owned enslaved workers.

____ 3. Van Buren avoided the press whenever possible.

____ 4. The Albany Regency was an organization of the Whig party in New York.

____ 5. People and states borrowing money too freely was one of the causes of the Panic of 1837.

Multiple Choice:

6. Which office did Van Buren never hold?
   A. Vice president
   C. Senator
   B. U.S. representative
   D. Secretary of state

7. Which of these were nicknames for Van Buren?
   A. Old Hickory
   C. Little Van
   B. Old Kinderhook
   D. Old Rough and Ready

8. Who lost to Van Buren in the election of 1836 but won in 1840?
   A. John Quincy Adams
   C. William Henry Harrison
   B. Andrew Jackson
   D. John C. Calhoun

Structured Response:

9. Where did Van Buren focus his attention during the Panic of 1837?

   _____

   _____

   _____

10. How did Van Buren's stance on slavery change throughout his lifetime?

   _____

   _____

   _____

   _____

   _____

WILLIAM HENRY HARRISON
(1773–1841, P. 1841)

William Henry Harrison was born in a three-story mansion into a wealthy Virginia family. He was tutored at home, then graduated from Hampden-Sidney College. He entered the army infantry in 1791. In 1795, he married the daughter of a wealthy farmer and built her a log cabin on a farm in Ohio. This log cabin later became part of a larger home, but it would become important as part of his presidential campaign years later. William Henry and Anna Harrison had ten children.

In 1799, Harrison was the Northwest Territory's delegate to Congress, and he convinced Congress to separate Ohio and Indiana. He was appointed by President John Adams as governor of the Indiana Territory in 1800. Earlier, he had opposed slavery, but now he sided with the majority of Indiana's settlers that since slavery was legal, citizens should have the right to own slaves.

Harrison tried to get Native Americans living in the territory to give up their land so whites could settle there. Tecumseh and his younger brother Tenskwatawa, who was called "the Prophet," organized the Shawnee and other Native Americans to fight against giving their land away. The Prophet's followers believed he could do anything, but it was Tecumseh who was a truly great leader.

In 1811, Governor Harrison, authorized by the U.S. government, formed an army of 1,000 men and moved toward the Native American camp at the Tippecanoe River. After Tecumseh left the camp to organize southern tribes, Harrison knew the time had come to strike. Urged on by the Prophet, the Native American warriors attacked Harrison's camp at dawn. It was a close battle, but it was soon reported as a great victory for the army. Afterward, people referred to Harrison as "Old Tip" or "Old Tippecanoe."

During the War of 1812, Harrison was made a brigadier general. He took command of the Army of the Northwest and recaptured Detroit from the British. Chasing the British-Native American force into Canada, Harrison's army won the Battle of the Thames, in which Tecumseh was killed. There was little fighting in the West after that; Harrison resigned and returned to his farm.

In 1816, Harrison was elected to the U.S. House. He became an Ohio state senator in 1819, a member of the U.S. Senate in 1825, and minister (ambassador) to Colombia in 1828. He became a Whig for the same reason many others did; he did not like Andrew Jackson. In 1836, he ran as a Whig for president against Van Buren and lost. He ran again in 1840.

The campaign of 1840 featured songs, jingles, parades, and barbecues. People, bitter over the Panic of 1837, put the blame on Van Buren. Appealing to the common man as the "log cabin and hard cider" candidate, Harrison and the Whigs portrayed Van Buren as sitting in splendor sipping fine French wine. The Whig campaign had a catchy phrase, "Tippecanoe and Tyler Too!," while the Democrats formed "O.K." clubs for "Old Kinderhook." Harrison easily won the election with 234 electoral votes to Van Buren's 60.

HARRISON AS PRESIDENT. Harrison's inaugural address was given outdoors on a cold, stormy day. It was the longest ever given, 105 minutes long and 8,455 words.

Harrison tired of Henry Clay pressuring him to appoint Clay people to high government offices. His most important appointment was Daniel Webster as secretary of state.

Perhaps weakened by exposure on Inauguration Day, the 68-year-old Harrison caught a cold a few weeks later. The cold turned into pneumonia, and he died April 4, 1841. He had been president for only a month.

Name: _____ Date: _____

Recalling Key Details

Directions: Answer the following questions using what you have learned from the reading selection.

Matching:

____ 1. The Whigs' campaign slogan for William Henry Harrison

____ 2. Democratic groups who supported Martin Van Buren

____ 3. Territory where Harrison was governor

____ 4. State where Harrison's log cabin and farm were

____ 5. Country where Harrison was an ambassador

A. Ohio

B. Indiana

C. Colombia

D. "O.K." clubs

E. "Tippecanoe and Tyler Too!"

Multiple Choice:

6. Which Native American, whom Harrison faced, was a truly great leader?
   A. The Prophet
   C. Tenskwatawa
   B. Sequoyah
   D. Tecumseh

7. In which battle was Tecumseh killed?
   A. Battle of the Thames
   C. Battle of Horseshoe Bend
   B. Battle at Tippecanoe River
   D. Battle at Detroit

8. Who did Harrison appoint to be secretary of state?
   A. Henry Clay
   C. Martin Van Buren
   B. Daniel Webster
   D. Andrew Jackson

Structured Response:

9. Why did Harrison support slavery in Indiana Territory?

_____

_____

_____

10. How did the Whig party's campaign for Harrison appeal to the common man?

_____

_____

_____

_____

JOHN TYLER
(1790–1862, P. 1841–1845)

Vice President John Tyler was at home in Virginia when he received word that President William Henry Harrison had died unexpectedly. He immediately went to Washington, D.C., and was sworn in by the chief justice of the U.S. Circuit Court at the Indian Queen Hotel. Tyler was the first vice president to become president because of the death of the president.

Tyler was born in 1790 on his family's plantation. Very little is known about his boyhood except for an incident when he was 11; he led a student revolt against a domineering teacher. He graduated from the College of William and Mary when he was 17 years old. Tyler became a lawyer when he was 21. He was first elected to the Virginia legislature in 1811 and to the U.S. House in 1816. He was elected governor of Virginia in 1825 and became a U.S. senator in 1827.

Tyler was a slaveholder himself and believed slavery was an issue for states to deal with and that the federal government could not interfere. He voted against the bill authorizing President Andrew Jackson to send federal troops to collect taxes in South Carolina. He opposed Jackson, but he disagreed with the majority of Whigs on most issues. However, the Whigs chose him for vice president in 1840 to win Southern support for the party. They had never dreamed that Tyler would be president.

TYLER AS PRESIDENT. From the beginning, Tyler had trouble establishing himself as "president," and not "acting president." His opponents sometimes called him "His Accidency." At his first cabinet meeting, Secretary of State Daniel Webster told him that Harrison had put every decision of the cabinet to a majority vote. Tyler said that he would seek their advice, but he would never be dictated to by his cabinet. If they agreed, they were welcome to stay in the cabinet; if not, they should resign. All except Webster resigned within a few weeks.

Tyler did not support high tariffs and internal improvements paid for by the federal government. The Whigs then turned against him. When Congress passed a bill creating a new Bank of the United States, he vetoed it. That night, an angry, rock-throwing mob surrounded the White House. Tyler passed out guns to the servants, but the crowd eventually left.

In 1843, the House voted on a resolution to impeach Tyler, "vice president acting as president," for the crimes of corruption and misconduct in office. The charges were rejected by a vote of 83 in favor, 127 opposed.

Tyler's first wife and the mother of his first eight children, Letitia, was suffering from a paralytic stroke when he became president, and she died in 1842. In 1844, he fell in love with a much younger woman, Julia Gardiner, and they married that year. She was a fine hostess and became well known for her entertaining.

Tyler favored annexing Texas, but many Northerners opposed admitting another slave state. When James K. Polk, who favored expansion, won the election of 1844, Congress approved annexing Texas three days before Tyler left office. Tyler and Julia returned to Virginia, where they raised a new family of seven more children. In 1861, he worked to keep the peace between North and South.

When Virginia left the Union in 1861, Tyler was elected to the Confederate House of Representatives but died before he could take his seat. The U.S. government made no official announcement of his death, the only time that has been done in U.S. history. It was not until 1911 that Congress appropriated money for a monument in his honor.

Name: _____ Date: _____

Recalling Key Details

Directions: Answer the following questions using what you have learned from the reading selection.

Matching:

____ 1. John Tyler opposed these taxes.

____ 2. Tyler did not want the federal government paying for these.

____ 3. Tyler vetoed this.

____ 4. Tyler's profession before he was elected to office

____ 5. Congress approved annexing this state just three days before Tyler left office.

A. high tariffs

B. lawyer

C. internal improvements

D. Bank of the United States

E. Texas

Multiple Choice:

6. Tyler was chosen to run as vice president because he would bring support from what group?
   - A. Northerners
   - B. New Englanders
   - C. Southerners
   - D. Businessmen

7. What group did Tyler say he would listen to but never be dictated to by?
   - A. Congress
   - B. The Southern states
   - C. The Supreme Court
   - D. His cabinet

8. When the Civil War began, which side did Tyler ultimately support?
   - A. The Union
   - B. The Confederacy
   - C. He left for Europe.
   - D. He remained neutral.

Structured Response:

9. Why do you think it might have been harder for Tyler to get much done when many people only thought of him as "acting president"?

_____

_____

_____

_____

10. What was unusual about Tyler's death?

_____

_____

_____

JAMES K. POLK
(1795–1849, P. 1845–1849)

James K. Polk was born in North Carolina in 1795, the son of a prosperous farmer. He graduated with honors from the University of North Carolina in 1818. He moved to Tennessee where he became a lawyer and a friend of Andrew Jackson.

In 1822, Polk was elected to the Tennessee legislature, and two years later, he was elected to the U.S. House. He only missed one day of House sessions in 14 years. In 1835, he was elected speaker of the house. He left the House in 1839 to become Tennessee's governor. He was not re-elected in 1841 and failed again in 1843.

At the Democratic Convention in 1844, Polk's name was put forth on the eighth ballot as a compromise candidate, and he received 44 votes. On the ninth ballot, he was chosen by all 266 delegates. He was a "dark horse" candidate who seemed to come out of nowhere. In fact, Polk had hoped to be chosen for vice president, but his powerful friends in the party proposed him for president when no one else held a clear majority.

Much of Polk's campaign and presidency was tied to the westward expansion of the United States. People began to think that it was the "manifest destiny" of the United States to spread from the Atlantic to the Pacific Ocean, and Polk agreed. Polk favored Texas annexation and expanding the U.S. claim to Oregon.

Polk's Whig opponent, Henry Clay, felt it was his time to be president after serving as a senator, speaker of the house, and secretary of state. He appealed to the East with his support for high tariffs and the West by favoring federal support for internal improvements. He opposed Texas annexation. Both Clay and Polk owned enslaved people, but Clay wanted to prevent the spread of slavery into new states and territories. Polk barely beat Clay with 38,000 more popular votes; in electoral votes, the majority was much greater, 170–105.

POLK AS PRESIDENT. Polk knew exactly what he wanted to accomplish and worked to get Congress to go along with his ideas. Congress reduced the tariff and created the Independent Treasury system, used until 1913 when the Federal Reserve System was created.

Some Democrats were willing to fight Great Britain for all of Oregon Country up to 54°40′ N latitude. Polk was willing to compromise by drawing the boundary at 49° N latitude. Britain backed down and agreed to the compromise.

Polk pushed the dispute with Mexico over the boundary of Texas until Congress declared war in 1846. Zachary Taylor's army scored victories in northern Mexico, while Winfield Scott captured Mexico City. Also in 1846, Americans in California staged the Bear Flag Revolt against Mexico. The U.S. navy and army secured victories over the Mexican forces there. Congress then had to decide whether or not the area gained in the war with Mexico would be open to slavery. The Wilmot Proviso, which would have prevented slavery in this new territory, was defeated in the Senate.

Sarah Polk was a popular first lady, and even his worst enemies found her charming. She was very devout, however, and she allowed no card playing, wine, or dancing in the White House. The couple had no children.

Polk only wished to serve one term as president and was happy to leave the presidency, having achieved most of his goals. Following Zachary Taylor's inauguration in March 1849, Polk and his wife took a tour of the South and moved back to Tennessee. However, he had become ill on the trip and died at his home, most likely of cholera, on June 15, 1849.

Name: _____   Date: _____

Recalling Key Details

Directions: Answer the following questions using what you have learned from the reading selection.

Matching:

_____ 1. Belief that the United States should stretch from the Atlantic to the Pacific Ocean

_____ 2. Disease that most likely killed James K. Polk

_____ 3. A little-known candidate who suddenly wins the race

_____ 4. The northern boundary for this U.S. territory was set at 49° N latitude

_____ 5. Uprising against Mexico in California

A. dark horse
B. manifest destiny
C. Oregon
D. cholera
E. Bear Flag Revolt

Multiple Choice:

6. Which office did James K. Polk never hold?
   A. U.S. representative
   C. Speaker of the house
   B. Governor
   D. U.S. senator

7. Which office did Henry Clay never hold?
   A. U.S. representative
   C. Speaker of the house
   B. Governor
   D. U.S. senator

8. What was created during Polk's administration to manage the federal money supply?
   A. Federal Reserve
   C. Independent Treasury
   B. First Bank of the United States
   D. Second Bank of the United States

Structured Response:

9. How could Congress have stopped the spread of slavery after the war with Mexico?

_____

_____

_____

10. What goals did Polk achieve while he was president?

_____

_____

_____

_____

_____

ZACHARY TAYLOR
(1784–1850, P. 1849–1850)

Zachary Taylor was born into a large and wealthy Virginia family. In 1785, the family moved to Kentucky in an area with no schools and no teachers. In 1808, Taylor entered the army, and in 1810, he was made a captain and married Margaret Smith. Margaret went wherever Zachary was stationed and never complained about the crude accommodations provided at army forts. Taylor served in campaigns against Native Americans, and in 1841, he became commander of the western division of the army. In 1844, he was posted in Louisiana and promoted to brevet (temporary) brigadier general. The Taylors had six children, three of which died of malaria.

By that time, Taylor was legendary for his manner of dressing like a farmer in a straw hat and baggy pants. Taylor's nickname was "Old Rough and Ready." He slept in simple tents and ate simple foods, and his men loved and respected him.

In 1846, his army was ordered to the Rio Grande by President James K. Polk. A patrol was attacked, and some of his men were killed. Polk used this incident to convince Congress that "American blood had been shed on American soil." Even before war with Mexico was declared, Taylor's army won two battles at Palo Alto and Resaca de la Palma. At Monterrey, Taylor's advancing army defeated a much larger Mexican force. At Buena Vista, while Taylor's army of 5,000 held its position, the Mexican force of 14,000 retreated with heavy casualties.

Taylor was a hero to the nation but was criticized by Polk. Since he had never voted, no one knew whether he was Whig or Democrat, but Taylor informed the Whigs that if they nominated him for president, he would accept. The letter from the Whig party informing Taylor he had been chosen came with postage due, so he refused to accept it. A second letter finally arrived a few weeks later.

In 1848, there were three candidates in the field: Taylor (Whig), Lewis Cass (Democrat), and Martin Van Buren (Free Soil). Taylor won the election with 1.36 million popular votes to Cass's 1.22 million votes. The electoral vote was 163–127. Van Buren only got 291,000 votes, but the Free Soil movement, which opposed slavery in the territories, was gaining momentum.

TAYLOR AS PRESIDENT. Since he had no political experience and was not well-informed on many issues, Taylor relied on Senator William Seward of New York to help guide him. Most of Taylor's cabinet opposed slavery expansion into territories. Even though he was a Southerner and slave owner himself, Taylor came out in favor of making California and New Mexico free states. The South was angry, many Southern Whigs left the party, and Southern members of Congress talked about secession (leaving the Union).

Henry Clay returned to the Senate in 1849 and began to work with others on a compromise between the North and South. This would become known as the Compromise of 1850. Its five main parts were: (1) California was to be admitted as a free state; (2) territorial governments were to be organized in New Mexico and Utah, with the people voting on the question of slavery; (3) the Texas-New Mexico boundary was to be settled in favor of New Mexico with Texas to receive $10 million; (4) the slave trade was to be ended in Washington, D.C.; and (5) a stronger fugitive slave law was to be put into effect. Taylor did not support the Compromise, but his views were ignored as Congress debated the issues Clay had proposed.

After presiding at the ceremony laying the cornerstone for the Washington Monument on July 4, 1850, Taylor suffered an unknown intestinal illness, possibly cholera or food poisoning, and died on July 9. Vice President Millard Fillmore then became president. Mrs. Taylor returned to Louisiana to live.

Name: _____ Date: _____

Recalling Key Details

Directions: Answer the following questions using what you have learned from the reading selection.

Fact/Opinion:

Write *F* if the statement is a fact or *O* if it is an opinion.

____ 1. Zachary Taylor was known for being a sloppy dresser.

____ 2. Taylor hadn't said whether he was a Democrat or Whig before 1848.

____ 3. Taylor was the best general since George Washington.

____ 4. Taylor shouldn't have been elected president since he didn't have any political experience.

____ 5. Taylor supported keeping slavery out of the new territories.

Multiple Choice:

6. An attack on Taylor's forces near which river was used to justify declaring war on Mexico?
   A. Colorado River
   B. Red River
   C. Arkansas River
   D. Rio Grande

7. In 1848, Martin Van Buren ran for president again, this time for which party that wanted to stop the spread of slavery?
   A. Whig
   B. Republican
   C. Free Soil
   D. Democratic

8. What was the legislation called that had five main parts dealing with slavery and the territory gained after the Mexican War?
   A. Missouri Compromise
   B. Compromise of 1850
   C. Kansas-Nebraska Act
   D. Treaty of Guadalupe Hidalgo

Structured Response:

9. Why might people vote for a military hero instead of an experienced politician or diplomat?

_____

_____

_____

10. Why was it important to deal with the question of slavery in the territory gained from Mexico?

_____

_____

_____

_____

MILLARD FILLMORE
(1800–1874, P. 1850–1853)

For the second time, a vice president became president because of the death of a president. The public knew even less about Fillmore than they had known about John Tyler. After he left office, the public quickly forgot him.

Millard was born in a log cabin in New York state, the son of poor farmers. Millard received very little schooling, but he was bright, and at 18 became a clerk at a lawyer's office. A year later, he became a lawyer. He married when he was 26. Millard and Abigail Fillmore had two children.

People saw in Fillmore the potential for a politician. He had been born in a log cabin, was good-looking, honest, and made friends easily. He joined the Anti-Masonic party, a group opposed to secret organizations. In 1828, he was elected to the New York legislature, where he proposed a law that would end imprisonment for debt. In 1831, he was elected to the U.S. House; he later became a Whig when that party was formed.

After Fillmore became chairman of the House Committee on Ways and Means, he wrote the tariff in 1842, which raised taxes on imported manufactured goods. He left the House in 1844, ran for governor, and lost. He became chancellor of the University of Buffalo in 1846. In 1848, the Whigs chose him for vice president, and when Zachary Taylor died in 1850, he became president.

FILLMORE AS PRESIDENT. Personally, Fillmore opposed slavery, but he feared a national disaster if the South was not satisfied. His whole cabinet resigned the day he took office; he asked them to stay for at least a month, but they stayed only one week. The people he appointed all favored the Compromise of 1850. As the different portions of the Compromise passed, he signed them. The North was quite angry with the new fugitive slave law, which required runaway slaves to be returned to their owners, but Fillmore was determined to enforce it.

The West was growing rapidly, and it became clear that a railroad to the Pacific would help it grow even faster. Fillmore worked with Senator Stephen Douglas to get grants for railroad construction. A strip across northern Mexico was bought for $10 million (the Gadsden Purchase) for the purpose of gaining the right of way for a southern railroad route.

Western Native American tribes gathered at Fort Laramie in 1851. Each tribe was given a large area of land, where they were promised they could live for all time. The government did not keep its word, and these areas became smaller as more settlers moved into the region.

In 1852, Commodore Matthew Perry sailed to Japan in an effort to open trade with that isolated nation. The fleet arrived in January 1853. An agreement was not signed until 1854. Even though the agreement was only to help shipwrecked sailors, it was the first crack in the door to trade between the United States and Japan; few realized its importance at the time.

When the Whig Convention met in 1852, the party passed over Fillmore and chose the Mexican War's other hero, General Winfield Scott, as its nominee. He was defeated by Franklin Pierce, who became president in 1853. Mrs. Fillmore died a few weeks after her husband left office. No more Whigs were ever elected president. In 1856, Fillmore ran for president on a combined Whig/Know-Nothing ticket (the Know-Nothings were against Catholics and immigrants). In that election, Fillmore carried only Maryland.

During the Civil War, Fillmore was critical of Lincoln and supported his Democratic opponent, George McClellan, in 1864. After McClellan's defeat, Fillmore never ventured into public life again. He died in 1874.

Name: _____ Date: _____

Recalling Key Details

Directions: Answer the following questions using what you have learned from the reading selection.

Matching:

____ 1. Millard Fillmore's profession before he became a politician

____ 2. State Fillmore represented in the U.S. House

____ 3. Tax on imported manufactured goods

____ 4. What the United States hoped to build across the Gadsden Purchase area

____ 5. A political party against Catholics and immigrants

A. tariff

B. railroad

C. Know-Nothing

D. New York

E. lawyer

Multiple Choice:

6. What law did Fillmore sign that was unpopular with the North?
   A. High tariff
   B. California statehood bill
   C. Gadsden Purchase
   D. Fugitive Slave Act

7. Commodore Matthew Perry was able to get the first agreement with what isolated country?
   A. China
   B. Russia
   C. Japan
   D. Korea

8. Who did Fillmore support during the presidential election of 1864?
   A. George McClellan
   B. Winfield Scott
   C. Abraham Lincoln
   D. Franklin Pierce

Structured Response:

9. Agreements signed at Fort Laramie promised Native American tribes a certain area of land. What actually happened to their land?

_____

_____

_____

10. What were some of the positive things that happened for the country during Fillmore's presidency?

_____

_____

_____

_____

FRANKLIN PIERCE
(1804–1869, P. 1853–1857)

At the 1852 Democratic convention, no candidate could get the two-thirds majority the party rules dictated. Finally after gaining some support as a dark horse candidate who could unite the party, Franklin Pierce was chosen as the presidential nominee on the 49th ballot.

Although not many in the general public knew who Pierce was, he seemed born to be a politician. Pierce's father had been a Revolutionary War general and a governor of New Hampshire. Franklin graduated from Bowdoin College, became a lawyer at 22, a member of the state legislature at 24, speaker of the state house at 26, a member of the U.S. House at 28, and a senator at 32. He was well liked and charming, but was known for spending too much time drinking. He was very agreeable and tried to please everyone. However, in 1842, he resigned from the Senate at his wife's request because she hated politics. In 1847, Pierce enlisted as a private to fight in the Mexican War. He was elected colonel of his regiment in February and was a brigadier general in March. He was in several battles, but his record was not impressive. He resigned from the army in 1848.

The campaign of 1852 centered on the qualities of the two candidates rather than their programs. The Whig candidate, Winfield Scott, had served his country well since the War of 1812. His victories in the Mexican War had forced Mexico to make peace. Pierce's record in the Mexican War was ridiculed by the Whigs, who charged he had fainted in two battles, become ill and gone to bed during the third, and missed the fourth by an hour. They also criticized his drinking.

In the election, Pierce carried 27 states and received 254 electoral votes. Scott only carried four states and received 42 electoral votes. This was the last full-scale presidential campaign for the Whigs.

Just before he became president, Pierce and his wife Jane were devastated by tragedy. They had already lost two of their three sons who had died while very young. The third son, eleven-year-old Bennie, was killed in a train accident as the family traveled through Massachusetts on January 6, 1853. Mrs. Pierce never fully recovered, and President Pierce began his term deeply depressed.

PIERCE AS PRESIDENT. The slavery issue continued to divide Congress and the nation. For his cabinet, Pierce chose only pro-slavery members. Among them was Jefferson Davis from Mississippi as secretary of war.

Pierce supported Senator Stephen Douglas' Kansas-Nebraska bill, which would create the territories of Kansas and Nebraska and let the people there decide whether to have slavery. This would effectively repeal the Missouri Compromise line of 36°30′ and outraged many Northerners. Pierce believed that the Constitution allowed slavery and that states had a right to allow it, no matter where they were located. The bill was finally passed, and in Kansas, pro-slave and anti-slave settlers clashed in battles that earned the territory the nickname of "Bleeding Kansas."

In 1856, the Democrats faced the Republican Party, which was formed in 1854 from members of the old Whig party, Free Soilers, and abolitionists—nearly all in free states. The Know-Nothing party were against Catholics and immigrants and were organized in both the North and South. Pierce wanted to be re-elected but could not even get the Democratic nomination.

After James Buchanan was elected, the Pierces went to Europe for nearly two years. When he returned, Pierce refused to run for president again. During the Civil War, he opposed Lincoln's policies and called the war "fearful, fruitless, fatal." This ruined his reputation. Pierce died in 1869.

Name: _____ Date: _____

Recalling Key Details

Directions: Answer the following questions using what you have learned from the reading selection.

Matching:

____ 1. Conflict where Franklin Pierce fought in the army
____ 2. Pierce's profession before being elected to office
____ 3. Pierce's father was a general in this war
____ 4. A little-known candidate selected to unite the party
____ 5. Windfield Scott was the last presidential candidate of this party

A. Revolutionary War
B. Mexican War
C. lawyer
D. Whig
E. dark horse

Multiple Choice:

6. Which office did Pierce never hold?
   A. U.S. senator
   B. U.S. representative
   C. Vice president
   D. Speaker of the New Hampshire state house

7. What caused the death of the Pierces' son, Bennie?
   A. Tuberculosis
   B. Epilepsy
   C. Horse-riding accident
   D. Train accident

8. In 1856, which new political party had support mostly in the north from those who were anti-slavery?
   A. Republican
   B. Democratic
   C. Know-Nothing
   D. Whig

Structured Response:

9. When the nation was so divided over slavery, why did Pierce support the Kansas-Nebraska bill?

_____
_____
_____
_____

10. Why did it seem like Pierce was born to be a politician?

_____
_____
_____
_____

JAMES BUCHANAN
(1791–1868, P. 1857–1861)

James Buchanan was born in a log cabin in western Pennsylvania in 1791. His Irish immigrant father ran a country store, and James learned arithmetic keeping records at the store. He graduated from Dickinson College in 1809, and studied law in Lancaster. He became a successful lawyer and was worth $300,000 when he became president. During the War of 1812, Buchanan enlisted as a private. He served in the Pennsylvania legislature from 1814 to 1816. He was engaged to be married, but the engagement was broken, the woman soon died, and Buchanan never married. He later adopted his sister's two daughters.

Buchanan was elected to the House of Representatives in 1820. In 1831, President Jackson chose him as minister to Russia, where he succeeded in making the first trade agreement with the Russian czar. He served as a U.S. senator from Pennsylvania from 1834 to 1845. Buchanan then served as President Polk's secretary of state and as President Pierce's minister to Great Britain.

The new Republican Party chose the famed explorer John C. Frémont as their candidate in 1856. Frémont opposed slavery's expansion into the territories. Many Democrats feared war would come if Frémont was elected. They said the South would secede (leave the Union). The Know-Nothings nominated Millard Fillmore for president. Since Buchanan had been in England during the troubles of recent years, the Democrats considered him an electable candidate and chose him to run with John C. Breckinridge from Kentucky as vice president. With many Southern friends, Buchanan had much more support than any of the other candidates. Buchanan carried 19 states with 174 electoral votes, Frémont won in 11 states with 114 electoral votes, and Fillmore carried one state with eight electoral votes. The Democrats controlled both houses of Congress.

BUCHANAN AS PRESIDENT. Buchanan wanted to hold the nation together, but he blamed abolitionists for creating fear in the South. Among those were Harriet Beecher Stowe, Reverend Henry Ward Beecher, and William Lloyd Garrison. Abolitionists were also smuggling slaves out of the South to Canada through the Underground Railroad.

Buchanan's troubles began when the Supreme Court handed down its decision in *Dred Scott v. Sandford.* The majority of the Court ruled that blacks were not citizens and could not bring cases to the federal courts. The Court also said the Missouri Compromise was unconstitutional. This meant slavery could spread into the territories.

In Kansas, pro-slavery and anti-slavery settlers had each set up a capital and elected legislatures. Buchanan sided with the pro-slavery legislature, even though it was unfairly chosen. Senator Stephen Douglas of Illinois split with Buchanan over this, and many other Democrats agreed with Douglas.

John Brown's attempt to cause a slave uprising by attacking the federal armory at Harper's Ferry, Virginia, in 1859, also added to tensions with the South.

Buchanan was not chosen to run again in 1860. Northern Democrats backed Stephen Douglas, and Southern Democrats backed John C. Breckinridge. The Republicans chose Abraham Lincoln, who had gained fame in his debates with Douglas during the Illinois senate race in 1858. The Constitutional Union party chose John Bell as their candidate.

After Lincoln won the election, South Carolina seceded in December 1860, and six other states followed before Buchanan left office in March. Buchanan argued that the states could not leave the Union, but he felt he did not have the power to make them stay. When his term was up, Buchanan returned home to Lancaster, Pennsylvania. He died there in 1868.

Name: _____ Date: _____

Recalling Key Details

Directions: Answer the following questions using what you have learned from the reading selection.

Matching:

_____ 1. Country where James Buchanan served as minister for President Jackson

_____ 2. Country where Buchanan served as minister for President Pierce

_____ 3. Party that chose Buchanan to run for president

_____ 4. Party that chose John C. Frémont to run for president

_____ 5. Those Buchanan blamed for creating fear in the South

A. Democratic

B. abolitionists

C. Republican

D. Great Britain

E. Russia

Multiple Choice:

6. Which person was not a famous abolitionist working to end slavery?
   A. Henry Ward Beecher
   B. Stephen Douglas
   C. William Lloyd Garrison
   D. Harriet Beecher Stowe

7. The Supreme Court decision in *Dred Scott v. Sandford* meant that what was unconstitutional?
   A. Kansas-Nebraska Act
   B. Slavery
   C. Missouri Compromise
   D. Abolitionists

8. Who attacked the federal armory at Harper's Ferry, Virginia, hoping to start a slave uprising?
   A. John Brown
   B. Henry Ward Beecher
   C. Stephen Douglas
   D. William Lloyd Garrison

Structured Response:

9. Who were the candidates for each party in the presidential race of 1860? Who won?

   _____

   _____

   _____

   _____

10. Why did Buchanan not interfere when South Carolina and six other states seceded from the Union?

   _____

   _____

   _____

ABRAHAM LINCOLN
(1809–1865, P. 1861–1865)

Abraham Lincoln is one of the most admired American presidents. Most of Lincoln's time and effort was spent on winning the Civil War, but out of this time also came changes that affected the future: chartering of railroads to the Pacific, homesteads for farmers in the West, and land set aside for colleges to teach agriculture and mechanics.

Abraham was born to Tom and Nancy (Hanks) Lincoln in a log cabin in Kentucky. His father was a hardworking man with no education. His mother died in 1818, and Tom then married Mrs. Sarah Johnston in 1819. There was limited opportunity for an education, but Abraham learned to read and borrowed books whenever he could. Most of his time was spent in hard work, often with an ax or plow. In 1830, the Lincolns moved to Illinois. Abraham worked as a country store clerk at New Salem and, for a short time, was a captain in the militia during the Black Hawk War. He bought a store with a partner; the store failed, and his share of the debt was $1,000. It took years to pay off the debt, but, by doing so, he earned the nickname of "Honest Abe."

Lincoln ran for the Illinois state legislature in 1834 on the Whig ticket and was reelected three times. In 1837, he wrote of his opinion of slavery, admitting it was legal but that it was "both injustice and bad policy." Also during this time, Lincoln studied law and became a lawyer in 1836. He moved to Springfield and eventually joined William Herndon in the law partnership that lasted the rest of Lincoln's life. In 1846, Lincoln was elected to the U.S. House of Representatives, but became unpopular by opposing the Mexican War. After his one term, he returned to practicing law.

Lincoln married Mary Todd, who had come to Springfield from Kentucky, in 1842 after a two-year courtship. She was lively, intelligent, ambitious, and temperamental. However, their marriage was not smooth, and Lincoln suffered from bouts of depression. Of their four sons, only one lived to be an adult.

Lincoln was the leading challenger to Stephen Douglas for the U.S. Senate seat from Illinois in 1858. He opposed the Kansas-Nebraska Act that Douglas had pushed through. The debates between Lincoln and Douglas were reported across the nation. Douglas won his Senate seat again, but Lincoln's reputation made him a contender for the Republican presidential nomination in 1860.

Lincoln defeated William Seward, Salmon Chase, and several native-son candidates (those supported only by their state delegations) at the Republican party's convention held in Chicago. In the national election, he won a majority of electoral votes, all from Northern states, defeating Stephen Douglas, John C. Breckinridge, and John Bell. As soon as his victory was announced, South Carolina prepared to secede from the Union, and by March 1861 when Lincoln became president, seven states had left the Union.

LINCOLN AS PRESIDENT. In his inaugural address, Lincoln said the Southern states would have to choose whether to make war or not, but that he had no choice in whether to defend "property and places" belonging to the federal government. When the South refused to allow supplies to be sent to Fort Sumter, in the harbor of Charleston, South Carolina, and Confederate guns opened fire on the federal fort, the Civil War began.

Lincoln and the war (1861–1863). To build up the army, Lincoln called on the governors to supply 75,000 men. Four more slave states left the Union. Four slave-holding border states

(Missouri, Kentucky, Maryland, and Delaware), managed to stay in the Union throughout the war. Many military leaders, like Colonel Robert E. Lee, also left the Union army rather than fight their Southern family members and friends.

Early victories for the Confederates hurt Lincoln's reputation as president. At the first and second battles at Bull Run, the Union army was defeated. Lee was now the commanding general of the Confederate army, and his forces defeated a string of Union generals. Though technically a victory for the Union, Antietam was the bloodiest battle of the war and there was great loss of life on both sides. In the West, the war was going better for the Union, with several victories for General Ulysses Grant, including a major victory at Shiloh in Tennessee.

Lincoln and slavery. During the early days of the war, as much as Lincoln disliked slavery, he resisted pressure to end it. He feared the border states might become so angry they would leave the Union, and he knew the Constitution said that private property (including enslaved people) could not be taken without just compensation.

By the summer of 1862, Lincoln knew he needed to end slavery. There were several reasons: (1) since foreign nations did not like slavery, he could get more cooperation from them if he freed the enslaved people; (2) black troops could help fill the ranks of the Union army; (3) many in the North had changed their minds about slavery and now wanted it ended; and (4) enslaved people might abandon the South if there was hope they would be free.

After the Union victory at Antietam in September 1862, Lincoln issued the preliminary Emancipation Proclamation. On New Year's Day 1863, the Emancipation Proclamation went into effect, but it only freed the enslaved people in areas held by Confederates. It was not until the Thirteenth Amendment was ratified in 1865, however, that slavery came to an end in every American state and territory.

In July 1863, Union victories at Vicksburg, Mississippi, and Gettysburg, Pennsylvania, helped to turn the tide in favor of the North. In November, a cemetery at the Gettysburg battle site was ready for dedication, and Lincoln gave a speech that became known as the Gettysburg Address. In it, he said the war was being fought "so that government of the people, by the people, and for the people shall not perish from the earth."

Lincoln then put Grant in command of all Union armies. Casualties went up, but Lincoln stood by Grant because he won battles.

The election of 1864. Lincoln felt he needed Democratic support to win, so he picked a Tennessee Democrat, Andrew Johnson, for vice president. The Democrats chose General George McClellan for president. Union victories helped Lincoln's campaign. Lincoln won the election, 212–21 in electoral votes and by over 400,000 popular votes.

Lincoln's second inaugural address in March 1865 was unusual in a nation that had been in bitter warfare for four years. As the war was coming to an end, Lincoln wanted the nation to unite in spirit, and asked for "malice toward none" and "charity for all."

War's end. Lee's troops put up stiff defenses in the last battles of the war, but with Union armies closing in, Lee retreated from Richmond and Petersburg, Virginia. He was cornered at Appomattox Courthouse, Virginia, where he surrendered to Grant on April 9, 1865.

News of Lee's surrender thrilled most Northerners, but it disturbed John Wilkes Booth, a famous actor who supported the Southern cause. He and a group of conspirators plotted to kill Lincoln, the vice president, and the secretary of state. Booth shot Lincoln at Ford's Theatre while he and Mary were attending a performance on the evening of April 14. Despite efforts to save his life, Lincoln died the next day. Booth was found and killed on April 26.

Name: _____ Date: _____

Recalling Key Details

Directions: Answer the following questions using what you have learned from the reading selection.

Matching:

____ 1. Asked for "malice toward none" and "charity for all"
____ 2. Freed enslaved people in Confederate territory
____ 3. Senate campaign events that made Lincoln famous
____ 4. Said the Southern states would have to choose whether to make war or not
____ 5. Said that government of, by, and for the people "shall not perish from the earth"

A. First Inaugural Address
B. Second Inaugural Address
C. Gettysburg Address
D. Emancipation Proclamation
E. Lincoln-Douglas Debates

Multiple Choice:

6. What did Abraham Lincoln call "both injustice and bad policy"?
   A. The Civil War
   B. Slavery
   C. The Mexican War
   D. Defending Fort Sumter

7. Which job did Lincoln never have?
   A. U.S. senator
   B. State representative
   C. U.S. representative
   D. Store clerk

8. Which battle was not a Union victory?
   A. Antietam
   B. Gettysburg
   C. Bull Run
   D. Shiloh

Structured Response:

9. What were the reasons Lincoln decided in the summer of 1862 to free the enslaved people in Confederate-held areas?

_____
_____
_____
_____

10. How did Lincoln die, and who was responsible?

_____
_____
_____

ANDREW JOHNSON
(1808–1875, P. 1865–1869)

Andrew Johnson was the first vice president to ever become president after a president had been assassinated. The nation was still deeply divided, and Johnson took strong stands on issues, which resulted in his impeachment and near-removal from office.

Andrew was born into a poor family in North Carolina. His father died when he was three years old, and he was apprenticed to a tailor when he was 14 years old. After two years under the abusive master, Andrew ran away and moved to Tennessee. He married Eliza McCardle when he was 18 and she was 16. She encouraged him to improve his reading. They had five children.

Johnson's small tailor shop in Greeneville, Tennessee, became a place for men to discuss politics. He worked his way up as an elected official from alderman to mayor to both houses of the state legislature. He was elected to the U.S. House in 1843, became governor of Tennessee in 1851, and was chosen for the U.S. Senate in 1857. Even though he was a slave owner, he did not always vote with Southerners in Congress. He was more concerned with helping poor farmers than rich slave owners, and he wanted a homestead law giving land to poor whites. In 1862, the Homestead Act was finally passed.

When Southern congressmen gave up their seats after Lincoln was elected, Johnson denounced secession as treason and went back to Tennessee to speak out against it. He had to escape to Kentucky to avoid arrest when Tennessee seceded. He was the only Southern congressman who did not resign his seat in the Union government. This impressed Lincoln, and he later appointed Johnson as military governor of Tennessee with the rank of brigadier general.

In 1864, the Republicans and War Democrats united in the National Union Party ticket. Lincoln chose Johnson to be vice president in the hope it would draw Democrats and border staters to the ticket. Johnson was never asked to change parties, and he remained a Democrat at heart.

Vice presidency. At Lincoln's inauguration, he was suffering from typhoid fever and drank some whiskey. During his speech in the hot Senate chamber, the liquor went to his head, and he was obviously intoxicated. Six weeks later, Johnson was president.

JOHNSON AS PRESIDENT. The first few weeks after Johnson came into office, attention focused on ending the war and punishing those involved in the Lincoln assassination. Johnson soon clashed with radical Republicans over pardoning Southerners, restoring government in the South, and what rights the formerly enslaved people should be given. He believed in a strong presidency and felt he should run the Reconstruction of the South while the Congressional Republicans felt they should be in charge now that the war was over.

Congress started limiting Johnson's powers, including the right to remove officeholders without the consent of the Senate. When Johnson vetoed this "Tenure of Office" bill, Congress overrode the veto. When Johnson tried to fire Secretary of War Stanton, the radicals in the House used the law to impeach Johnson. In the Senate trial to remove him from office, Johnson escaped being convicted and removed by one vote.

Johnson's great achievement in foreign policy was buying Alaska from Russia for $7.2 million.

In 1875, Johnson returned to the Senate, representing Tennessee, but his stay was brief. He died later in the year.

Name: _____ Date: _____

Recalling Key Details

Directions: Answer the following questions using what you have learned from the reading selection.

Matching:

____ 1. Andrew Johnson's occupation before entering politics

____ 2. State where Johnson served as representative, governor, and senator

____ 3. Johnson's political party

____ 4. Territory that was purchased from Russia during Johnson's administration

____ 5. Label the Republicans in Congress were given during this time

A. Alaska

B. Democratic

C. Radical

D. tailor

E. Tennessee

Multiple Choice:

6. What was one of Johnson's main goals while in the U.S. House and Senate?
   A. Outlaw slavery
   B. Secede from the Union
   C. Enrich slave owners
   D. Pass a homestead law

7. Johnson was the first person to become president due to what?
   A. Impeachment
   B. Assassination
   C. Incompetence
   D. Popular vote

8. The Tenure of Office Act required the president to get whose approval before he could remove someone from office?
   A. The House
   B. The Supreme Court
   C. The Senate
   D. The vice president

Structured Response:

9. Why did Lincoln choose Johnson to be his vice-presidential running mate?

   _____

   _____

   _____

10. What process did Johnson and Congress each think they should be in charge of after the war?

   _____

   _____

   _____

ULYSSES S. GRANT
(1822–1885, P. 1869–1877)

Grant was born in Ohio and named Hiram Ulysses Grant. In 1839, when he was enrolled at the military academy at West Point, his name was mistakenly listed as Ulysses Simpson Grant. He preferred that to the initials H.U.G., and from then on was U.S. Grant. After graduating in 1843, he was appointed a brevet (temporary) second lieutenant in infantry. He was stationed outside St. Louis and met Julia Dent, whom he later married in 1848. The Grants had three sons and one daughter.

Grant fought during the Mexican War under Taylor and Scott, and by war's end, he was a brevet captain. While stationed in the Pacific Northwest, Grant's commanding officer found him drunk. He told him to resign or face court martial. Grant resigned to avoid hurting Julia's reputation. Grant then tried farming outside St. Louis, but failed. He also worked in his father's leather shop.

When the Civil War began in 1861, the army was not interested in him at first, but in June 1861, he was appointed a colonel in the 21st Illinois Volunteers. In August, he was made a brigadier general of troops in Illinois and Missouri; then his career took off. He won well-publicized victories for the Union at Forts Henry and Donelson in Tennessee. Promoted to major general, he won at the Battle of Shiloh in Tennessee and then laid siege to the Confederate stronghold at Vicksburg, Mississippi. After a victory at Chattanooga,Tennessee, President Lincoln named Grant lieutenant general in charge of all Union troops. A long series of bloody battles followed as Grant tangled with the Confederate General Robert E. Lee. Finally, Lee surrendered to Grant at Appomattox Courthouse, Virginia, on April 9, 1865.

Grant easily won the Republican nomination for president in 1868. Running with him was Schuyler Colfax, Speaker of the House. The Democratic candidate, Horatio Seymour, carried only eight states. The popular vote was much closer; Grant won with only a 300,000-vote margin.

GRANT AS PRESIDENT. Unlike Johnson, Grant was willing to let Congress lead in making laws. He often chose friends for high positions, but many of them were corrupt. Grant's brother-in-law was even involved in a plot to corner the gold market. A positive note during Grant's first administration was the completion of the transcontinental railroad to California in 1869.

The public stood by Grant after his first term, and he was reelected in 1872, defeating the Democratic candidate, Horace Greeley. He won the electoral vote 286 to 66 and the popular vote by over 750,000 votes.

However, in 1873, a major financial panic occurred, closing businesses and causing mass unemployment. Then more scandals involving the Union Pacific railroad, the Whiskey Ring, and bribery of government officials in Congress and Grant's administration became known.

Reconstruction was not progressing well in the South. The secret terror organization, the Ku Klux Klan (KKK), terrorized African Americans who tried to vote. Union troops could not control the frequent riots.

Grant did not run for president again in 1876. After leaving office, the Grants went on a long trip around the world and were greeted as heroes. In 1884, he lost most of his money to a bank swindler. Dying from cancer and desperate to provide an income for his wife, Grant wrote his autobiography. He died on July 23, 1885. The book form of the autobiography was published after his death by author Mark Twain. It became a best seller, and Grant's family earned $450,000 from it in the first two years.

Name: _____ Date: _____

Recalling Key Details

Directions: Answer the following questions using what you have learned from the reading selection.

Matching:

____ 1. Where Ulysses S. Grant received military training

____ 2. Action that would have put Grant on trial for drunkenness
        if he had not resigned from the army

____ 3. Where Grant first returned to military service in the Civil War

____ 4. State where the Union victories at Fort Henry, Fort Donelson,
        Shiloh, and Chattanooga took place

____ 5. Site where General Lee surrendered to Grant

A. court martial

B. West Point

C. Appomattox
   Courthouse

D. Illinois

E. Tennessee

Multiple Choice:

6. Which was not a scandal during Grant's administration?
   A. Teapot Dome
   B. Whiskey Ring
   C. Attempt to corner the gold market
   D. Union Pacific railroad

7. What happened in 1873 that set the nation back?
   A. The Civil War ended
   B. Grant was elected president
   C. A financial panic occurred
   D. The transcontinental railroad was completed

8. Which organization was terrorizing African Americans in the South?
   A. The Union army
   B. The Ku Klux Klan
   C. The Freedmen's Bureau
   D. The carpetbaggers

Structured Response:

9. Grant was a general who had little experience with politics. How did this show in his time in office?

   _____

   _____

   _____

   _____

10. Why did Grant want to write his autobiography?

   _____

   _____

   _____

RUTHERFORD B. HAYES
(1822–1893, P. 1877–1881)

Rutherford B. Hayes was born in Ohio in 1822; shortly after his birth, his father died. He graduated from Kenyon College in 1842 and attended Harvard Law School. He moved to Cincinnati, where his law career was very successful. He met and eventually married Lucy Webb; their marriage produced a daughter and seven sons.

Hayes was a Whig until the Republican party formed. When the Civil War came, he enlisted as a major and ended the war as a major general of volunteers. He was in the thick of battles and was wounded five times. In 1864, he was elected to the U.S. House, so he resigned from the army. In 1867, he left Congress to serve as governor of Ohio. He took the unpopular position that African Americans should be allowed to vote.

As governor (1867–1871), Hayes pushed for civil service reforms, voter registration to prevent voter fraud, and improvement in conditions in prisons and insane asylums. He established railroad regulation and granted approval of the Fifteenth Amendment. In 1872, he ran unsuccessfully for the U.S. House. In 1875, Hayes won a third term as governor.

In 1876, the Republican Convention chose Hayes as their candidate for president. Hayes had been honest throughout his career and was the safest choice to face the Democrats. The Democratic choice was Samuel Tilden, governor of New York, who had cleaned up corruption in his state. Both Hayes and Tilden wanted to end Reconstruction, and they favored civil service reform.

When the votes were counted, Tilden had 184 electoral votes and Hayes had 165. However, there were irregularities in three southern states with 20 more electoral votes. Ballots had disappeared, ballot boxes had been stuffed, and voters had been threatened. Each party was sure their candidate had won.

To solve the problem, Congress created the Electoral Commission. It consisted of seven Democrats, seven Republicans, and one independent. When the independent Justice David Davis was appointed the governor of Illinois, Republican Justice Joseph Bradley was appointed to take his place, giving the Republicans a majority. After investigating the returns in South Carolina, Louisiana, and Florida, the Commission concluded by an eight to seven vote in each case that Hayes had won. The totals were 185 for Hayes to 184 for Tilden. Congress finally declared Hayes the winner on March 2, 1877, two days before the president was to be inaugurated.

HAYES AS PRESIDENT. Democrats felt cheated, but Hayes appointed able and honest men to his cabinet, and he withdrew federal troops from the South as he had promised. White Democrats took charge in all Southern states. In 1877, Hayes issued an executive order forbidding federal employees from taking part in political organizations.

Since Hayes and his wife were active in the temperance movement, no alcohol was served at White House gatherings. Hayes' wife was referred to as "Lemonade Lucy." One of her contributions was the hosting of the Easter egg roll on the White House lawn.

Party leaders who depended on the spoils system were very unhappy with Hayes, as were those Californians who wanted the government to stop Chinese from immigrating to the United States. After workers rioted in several cities, Hayes sent troops to restore order.

After his term, Hayes said: "No one ever left the presidency with less disappointment, fewer heartburnings or more general content than I do." His wife died in 1889, and he died in 1893.

Name: _____ Date: _____

Recalling Key Details

Directions: Answer the following questions using what you have learned from the reading selection.

Matching:

____ 1. State where Rutherford B. Hayes was governor   A. African Americans

____ 2. Hayes' rank when he left the army   B. voter registration

____ 3. What Hayes wanted to cut down on voter fraud   C. major general

____ 4. Group that Hayes wanted to give the vote   D. Ohio

____ 5. Hayes wanted this type of reform to cut down on granting   E. civil service
           positions in government through the spoils system

Multiple Choice:

6. Which of these was not a state where there were thought to be voting irregularities in 1876?
     A. Florida   B. South Carolina
     C. Louisiana   D. Missouri

7. Who decided the election of 1876?
     A. The Senate   B. The voters
     C. The House's Electoral Commission   D. The Electoral College

8. When Reconstruction was ended in the South, who took over in those states?
     A. White Democrats   B. African-American Republicans
     C. White Republicans   D. An integrated Democratic Party

Structured Response:

9. Why was it important for both parties to run candidates known for honesty in 1876?

     _____

     _____

     _____

     _____

10. Why did the Democrats feel like they had been cheated out of the presidency in 1876?

     _____

     _____

     _____

     _____

     _____

JAMES GARFIELD
(1831–1881, P. 1881)

James Garfield was born in 1831 in a log cabin on the Ohio frontier. His father died when he was two years old. As a boy, James worked for farmers in the area and attended public school. When he was 16, he left home and worked on a lake schooner and then on the canal as a driver and helmsman. Garfield attended college and taught in a rural school. He became president of Western Reserve Eclectic Institute (now Hiram College) in Ohio where he had been a student. He loved languages and taught Latin, Greek, and German, as well as history and English. In addition to teaching, he was a Disciples of Christ preacher. In 1859, he married Lucretia Rudolph and became a state senator. The Garfields had seven children. He also studied law and passed the bar exam in 1860.

When the Civil War came, Garfield took command as colonel of the 42nd Ohio Volunteers. He knew nothing about military organization and strategy, but he worked hard and learned quickly. He won his first battle against a West Point graduate and was promoted to brigadier general. In 1862, Garfield was elected to the U.S. House while continuing to serve in the army. He entered the House in 1863 and was appointed to the Committee on Military Affairs. In September, he became a major general but resigned from the army in December to take his seat in the House.

Garfield, together with Speaker James G. Blaine, led the party during the Grant administration. Garfield served on major committees, and he had a reputation for honesty and hard work. By 1880, he was House minority leader.

Going into the election of 1880, the Republican Party was split between a group called "Stalwarts," who favored nominating former President Grant, and the "Half-breeds" who favored Blaine. Garfield was a Blaine supporter. Neither man could get enough support to win the nomination. Then on the 34th ballot, a few votes were cast for Garfield. He protested that his name had been mentioned without his consent. Garfield was chosen on the 36th ballot, and he was genuinely stunned. For vice president, the convention chose Chester Arthur.

The Democratic candidate, Winfield Hancock, had been a military hero, and had won great praise for setting up the defenses at Gettysburg. He had little political record and few enemies in the party. Both parties were guilty of dirty politics, accusing Hancock of cowardice and Garfield of corruption. The election was very close. Garfield beat Hancock by only 10,000 popular votes. His electoral vote majority was much higher, 214–155.

GARFIELD AS PRESIDENT. Garfield's main problem as president was the split in the Republican Party and the choice of men for high positions. Garfield clashed with Stalwart leader, Senator Roscoe Conkling of New York, when Garfield chose Blaine to be secretary of state and a Blaine supporter as customs collector for the Port of New York. Conkling and the other New York senator, Tom Platt, resigned. To their surprise, they were not reelected by the legislature. Garfield had made an important point, establishing the principle that appointments are the choice of the president, not the senators.

As Garfield walked through the Washington railroad station on July 2, 1881, he was shot by a disappointed office seeker, Charles Guiteau. As Guiteau was being wrestled down, he shouted out: "I am a Stalwart, and now Arthur is president." Garfield lingered as doctors tried to save him, but he eventually died of his wounds on September 19, 1881. Guiteau was found guilty of murder and hanged in 1882.

Name: _____ Date: _____

Recalling Key Details

Directions: Answer the following questions using what you have learned from the reading selection.

True/False:

Write *T* if the statement is true or *F* if it is false.

_____ 1. James Garfield was born in a log cabin and was uneducated.

_____ 2. Garfield served in the U.S. House while he was also in the army during the Civil War.

_____ 3. The division between the Stalwarts and Half-breeds caused trouble for the Republicans.

_____ 4. The Democrat Winfield Hancock lost the presidential election because it was proven he was a coward.

_____ 5. Garfield died a day after being shot by Charles Guiteau.

Multiple Choice:

6. Who was Garfield's vice president?
   - A. Roscoe Conkling
   - B. James G. Blaine
   - C. Chester Arthur
   - D. Tom Platt

7. Which profession did Garfield not have during his life?
   - A. Physician
   - B. Teacher
   - C. Lawyer
   - D. Canal boat helmsman

8. Who did the Stalwart Republicans want to run for president?
   - A. James G. Blaine
   - B. Winfield Hancock
   - C. James Garfield
   - D. Ulysses S. Grant

Structured Response:

9. By standing up to Conkling, what point did Garfield make?

_____

_____

_____

_____

10. How was Garfield's death related to the split in the Republican party?

_____

_____

_____

_____

_____

CHESTER ARTHUR
(1830–1886, P. 1881–1885)

Chester Arthur was born in Fairfield, Vermont. His father was an Irish-born Baptist preacher, and the family moved frequently, finally settling in Schenectady, New York. Chester taught school while helping pay his way through Union College. He continued teaching while he studied law and became a lawyer in 1854. He was a successful lawyer and married Ellen Herndon, the daughter of a naval officer, in 1859. The couple had three children, one of whom died in childhood.

In 1860, the governor of New York appointed Arthur quartermaster general of the state as a political favor. When the Civil War began, he was put in charge of feeding, housing, and supplying army recruits who were passing through New York City. He carried out his duties well, and during the war, he made friends with many important people and began to move up in Republican politics.

Offering bribes to government employees and officials became common when businessmen needed a friendly law or a government contract to get ahead of the competition. Corrupt party machines were present in both the major parties. In New York, the Tammany Hall Democratic politicians competed against the Roscoe Conkling Republican machine. Conkling had gotten Arthur appointed the collector of customs for the Port of New York during the Grant administration. The job paid well and gave 1,300 jobs to loyal party workers. Arthur was also the chairman of the Republican state committee. However, when President Hayes was elected and ordered that no federal employee could engage in politics, Arthur refused to resign, claiming that he had done nothing that wasn't common practice. The president fired him in July 1878.

In 1880, Conkling was chosen for the Senate. He led the Stalwarts (Grant supporters) at the Republican Convention of 1880. After James Garfield, a Half-breed (an anti-Grant reformer) won the nomination, a Stalwart leader suggested Arthur for vice president to gain Stalwart support. Conkling told Arthur to refuse the offer, but Arthur accepted it anyway. After Garfield won, most people still considered Arthur a Conkling puppet.

Garfield appointed Reform Republicans to federal jobs in New York over the protests of Conkling. Then came Charles Guiteau's shooting of the president, and his statement: "I am a Stalwart, and now Arthur is president." For weeks, Garfield's health declined. During that time, there were no cabinet meetings or other official functions, and then on September 19, 1881, the sad news came that Garfield had died.

ARTHUR AS PRESIDENT. Arthur surprised those who thought he would be guided by Conkling. Arthur was careful to choose able Republicans for office and ignored most of Conkling's requests. The assassination of Garfield caused a public demand for an end to the spoils system of doling out government jobs. In 1883, Democrats gained control of Congress and passed the Pendleton Civil Service Act. It created a Civil Service Commission; examinations were now required for about ten percent of government jobs. It was the beginning of the end of the spoils system. Arthur strongly supported the Pendleton Act.

During Arthur's presidency, mail service was improved, and postage stamps were dropped from three cents to two cents. Congress appropriated money for new steel ships to replace the old wooden ships of the Civil War era. Major improvements were made at the White House, and dinners and social events returned. Arthur's wife had died before he became president, but he and his sister were fine hosts.

Arthur was not nominated for reelection in 1884, and he died in 1886.

Name: _____ Date: _____

Recalling Key Details

Directions: Answer the following questions using what you have learned from the reading selection.

Matching:

____ 1. Job where Chester Arthur was in charge of feeding, clothing, and supplying New York army recruits

____ 2. Job where Arthur worked at the Port of New York and oversaw 1,300 employees

____ 3. Practice of giving government jobs to those who support an officeholder politically

____ 4. Republicans who were Grant supporters in 1880

____ 5. Reform Republicans who were against Grant in 1880

A. spoils system

B. Half-breeds

C. collector of customs

D. quartermaster general

E. Stalwarts

Multiple Choice:

6. Who was the head of the Republican political machine in New York?
   - A. Boss Tweed
   - B. Roscoe Conkling
   - C. Chester Arthur
   - D. James Garfield

7. Who fired Arthur from his job at the Port of New York?
   - A. President Hayes
   - B. Senator Conkling
   - C. President Grant
   - D. President Garfield

8. What law started reforms in the way government jobs were filled?
   - A. Sherman Antitrust Act
   - B. Pendleton Civil Service Act
   - C. Homestead Act
   - D. Kansas-Nebraska Act

Structured Response:

9. Why did Garfield's assassination cause a public demand for an end to the spoils system?

_____

_____

_____

_____

10. What were some of the accomplishments of the Arthur presidency?

_____

_____

_____

© Mark Twain Media, Inc., Publishers

GROVER CLEVELAND
(1837–1908, P. 1885–1889, 1893–1897)

Grover Cleveland was born in New Jersey, the son of a Presbyterian minister. His father died when he was 16. An uncle in Buffalo, New York, got him a job in a law firm. Cleveland was very determined and often worked all night without sleep. He did not like anything that wasted time, which included a social life. He postponed marriage until much later in life.

When the Civil War came, he hired a substitute to fight for him. This was perfectly legal, and he explained he did it because he supported his widowed mother. He was a loyal Democrat, and in 1862, he was named as a ward supervisor, then an assistant district attorney. He ran for district attorney in 1865; from that time until 1870, he worked at building up his law practice. Cleveland was elected sheriff of Buffalo County in 1871. He did not believe in making others do the difficult jobs, so he performed two hangings himself. After three years, he returned to private law practice.

In 1881, Buffalo reformers wanted to find a candidate for mayor who not only had political experience but was honest. Cleveland was elected, and as mayor, he rejected costly street cleaning and sewer contracts. In 1882, Cleveland was elected governor of New York with the motto: "A public office is a public trust." He did not allow the passing of costly spending bills that would help special interests. He refused to work with the Tammany Hall Democratic machine. He was now beginning to draw national support from reformers.

The Republican Convention met first in 1884, and the party quickly chose James G. Blaine, the most famous party leader of the time. However, Blaine's reputation had been tarnished by charges that he had received bribes from railroads. The Democrats chose Grover Cleveland, a man noted for his honesty. As soon as Cleveland was chosen, Reform Republicans, called "mugwumps," switched parties to support him.

The 1884 campaign. The campaign became the dirtiest to date. Democrats chanted: "Blaine, Blaine, James G. Blaine! The continental liar from the state of Maine." Then Republicans discovered that Cleveland had paid child support to an alcoholic widow and her son, claiming this was his illegitimate child. When Cleveland was asked what to do about the charge, he said: "Tell the truth." He acknowledged the possibility that the boy was his child. Opponents made up jokes about him, but others supported him because he had not lied.

Blaine lost support from many Catholics when he failed to speak out against a supporter who said that a vote for Cleveland was a vote for "rum, Romanism (Catholic Church), and rebellion." Blaine also spoke about "Republican prosperity" to a group of wealthy supporters, which didn't sit well with those going through hard times due to the financial depression.

The election was very close, but Cleveland won 217–184 in electoral votes; in New York state, he won by only 1,100 votes.

CLEVELAND AS PRESIDENT (first term). Cleveland's motto could have been: "When in doubt, say NO!" An example of this was his attitude toward veteran pensions. He had not served in the war, and Republican politicians were quick to point that out. He turned down individual pensions that had no merit. However, he also vetoed pensions for all veterans with disabilities, whether they had been disabled during the war or after. The pension issue probably hurt him in 1888.

Because the government was taking in more money than it spent, Cleveland recommended cutting the taxes on imports. When advisors warned him this would hurt him in Northern industrial states, he answered: "What is the use of being elected and reelected unless you stand for something?"

Public lands were being used by lumber companies and cattle ranchers. The government ordered cattle off government land and stopped lumbering operations. This policy change hurt Cleveland in the West.

Cleveland didn't show much imagination in creating new programs. The building of a new navy had started with Arthur; it was continued by Cleveland's secretary of the navy. The Interstate Commerce Act was passed in 1887 and gave the government the power to regulate interstate railroads.

In Cleveland's personal life, the biggest change was getting married. The bride was 21-year-old Frances Folsom, his law partner's daughter. She had become Cleveland's ward upon her father's death. They were married in the White House while John Philip Sousa's band played the wedding march. Cleveland was easier to get along with after the marriage, and he even took more vacations. He still worked long hours, going to bed between 2:00 and 3:00 A.M. Grover and Frances had five children, including Ruth, nicknamed Baby Ruth who was a darling of the press, and Esther, the first child of a president to be born in the White House.

After losing the election of 1888 to Republican Benjamin Harrison, Cleveland told the White House staff to take care of the furnishings. He wanted everything the same when he returned four years later.

CLEVELAND AS PRESIDENT (second term). Cleveland faced some tough problems during his second term, including economic collapse and labor strikes. Cleveland took charge of everything, answered the White House phone himself, and did not use secretaries. However, as new problems arose, Cleveland unfortunately used old methods to meet them, which did not work.

Much of the economic growth of the 1870–1890 period had been in railroad construction. As railroads either completed construction or could not borrow enough money to finish laying track, this affected industries like steel and coal that depended on railroads for much of their business. Unemployment spread; about 2.5 million workers lost their jobs. Even those who had money stopped spending. Jacob Coxey, a reformer, led an "army" of about 400 tired and hungry unemployed men to hold a demonstration in Washington. Coxey was arrested for walking on the White House lawn.

Workers at Pullman's Railroad Car factory had their wages cut, and they went on strike. They were supported by American Railway Union workers who refused to attach Pullman cars to trains. Attorney General Richard Olney persuaded Cleveland to crack down on the workers. Accused of interfering with the transport of mail, the union was ordered back to work. When the strike continued, the union president, Eugene Debs, was sent to prison for six months.

Cleveland provided little leadership in solving the economic crisis. Instead of spending money to help the unemployed or listening to worker complaints, Cleveland said the financial crisis was caused by too much money in circulation. The government stopped buying silver to make money. With tax revenue dropping, Cleveland built up the gold supply by selling bonds, and turned to the big banker, J. P. Morgan, for help.

Many Americans were outraged. One of these, William Jennings Bryan, attacked Cleveland policies at the Democratic Convention in 1896, and he became the party candidate for president. The Republicans chose William McKinley as their nominee.

After his term ended, Cleveland moved to Princeton, New Jersey. There was some talk of him running again in 1904, but he made no effort to win the nomination. He died in 1908.

. City where Cleveland began practicing law

. Cleveland paid this to an alcoholic widow and her son

. child support

6C. Civil War

6D. Buffalo

4E. bribes

1seoul

Name: _____ Date: _____

Recalling Key Details

Directions: Answer the following questions using what you have learned from the reading selection.

Matching:

____ 1. Grover Cleveland hired a substitute to fight for him during this
____ 2. City where Cleveland began practicing law
____ 3. Blaine was charged with receiving these from railroads
____ 4. Cleveland paid this to an alcoholic widow and her son
____ 5. Frances Folsom was made this after her father's death

A. Cleveland's ward
B. child support
C. Civil War
D. Buffalo
E. bribes

Multiple Choice:

6. Which job did Cleveland never have?
   A. Sheriff
   B. Governor
   C. Vice president
   D. Mayor

7. What leader of an unemployed "army" was arrested for walking on the White House lawn?
   A. J.P. Morgan
   B. Eugene Debs
   C. William Jennings Bryan
   D. Jacob Coxey

8. Cleveland wanted to build up the government's supply of what by selling bonds?
   A. Silver
   B. Paper money
   C. Gold
   D. Copper

Structured Response:

9. What were some of the groups who turned against Cleveland due to his policies?

_____
_____
_____
_____

10. How did the slow-down of railroad construction lead to the economic crisis?

_____
_____
_____
_____

BENJAMIN HARRISON
(1833–1901, P. 1889–1893)

Benjamin Harrison was the grandson of William Henry Harrison, and he was born on his grandfather's estate in Ohio in 1833. He graduated from Miami University (Ohio) in 1852 and married Caroline Lavinia Scott in 1853. They had three children. He studied law and then set up his law practice in Indianapolis, Indiana, in 1854. He joined the Republican Party because of the slavery issue and soon became one of its most effective public speakers.

Harrison served well in the army during the Civil War, including with Sherman in the battles around Atlanta. He left the army in 1865 as a brevet (temporary) brigadier general.

Harrison returned to his law practice and family. He was active in Republican politics, and entered the U.S. Senate in 1880 but lost his seat in 1886 when the Democrats took control of Indiana's legislature. James G. Blaine suggested that Harrison be the party nominee for president in 1888. He was chosen on the eighth ballot. The Democrats ran Grover Cleveland again.

Much of the support for Harrison's campaign came from wealthy backers. Harrison did his campaigning from his front porch. Groups would come, he would say a few words, and they would leave. Cleveland did not campaign and would not let cabinet members campaign for him. Harrison won the electoral vote 233–168, but Cleveland won the popular vote by 100,000.

HARRISON AS PRESIDENT. Harrison chose competent people for his administration, including James G. Blaine as secretary of state. However, the real leader of the government for his first two years was Speaker of the House Thomas ("Czar") Reed.

Republicans were eager to pass veterans' pensions and high tariffs. Under the new pension plan, any man who had served 90 days and was now physically or mentally disabled was eligible for a pension. The widows and children of veterans also received pensions. The McKinley tariff of 1890 was the highest tax on imports yet. Its taxes were set by American industries to keep foreign competition out. Businesses and workers in industrial states favored it, while consumers in farm states opposed it. The Sherman Silver Purchase Act was also passed to guarantee the government would buy more silver to be made into coins.

In 1890, Congress passed the Sherman Antitrust Act. It defined as a trust "any contract or combination in restraint of trade." Reformers thought this was an important first step, but the law was almost impossible to enforce.

The White House was renovated during Harrison's term. Electric lights were installed, but after a few shocks, Harrison told his family to let the staff turn them on and off. If they forgot, the lights stayed on all night.

Government was spending $989 million, and people started calling it the "billion-dollar Congress." Reed said this was a billion-dollar country and needed the money. The public disagreed. The Democrats took control of the House in 1890, and for his last two years as president, Harrison achieved very little.

Cleveland returns. In 1892, Cleveland ran for president again and won easily over Harrison; 277–145 in electoral votes, and by 380,000 in popular votes. The new Populist Party's James B. Weaver received 22 electoral votes. Harrison went back to private law practice, made a fortune, and wrote books. His first wife died in 1892, he remarried in 1896, and had another child in 1897. He died in 1901.

Name: _____ Date: _____

Recalling Key Details

Directions: Answer the following questions using what you have learned from the reading selection.

Matching:

_____ 1. Any contract or combination in restraint of trade

_____ 2. A tax on imports

_____ 3. Where Harrison did his campaigning for president

_____ 4. Improvement to the White House that Harrison wouldn't touch

_____ 5. A payment to someone who had served in the military and was mentally or physically disabled

A. front porch

B. pension

C. tariff

D. trust

E. electric lights

Multiple Choice:

6. Who was actually in control of the government for the first two years of Harrison's presidency?

   A. James G. Blaine

   B. William McKinley

   C. Grover Cleveland

   D. Thomas Reed

7. The McKinley tariff helped protect American industries from what?

   A. Investors

   B. Sales tax

   C. Foreign competition

   D. Minimum wage laws

8. Increased spending partly due to paying veterans' pensions and buying silver for coins led to this nickname for the Congress during Harrison's term.

   A. "trust-busting Congress"

   B. "spend-thrift Congress"

   C. "bankrupt Congress"

   D. "billion-dollar Congress"

Structured Response:

9. How was the campaign for president in 1888 between Harrison and Cleveland different from the campaigns we are used to today?

_____

_____

_____

_____

10. Why were the Democrats able to take control of Congress in 1890?

_____

_____

_____

WILLIAM McKINLEY
(1843–1901, P. 1897–1901)

William McKinley was born in Ohio in 1843. He only had one year of college before becoming ill. Then he taught school and was a post office clerk. When the Civil War came, he enlisted in the 23rd Ohio Volunteer Infantry Regiment, serving under Rutherford B. Hayes. McKinley left the army as a major. After the war, McKinley became a lawyer and was active in Republican politics. He married Ida Saxton in 1871, and the couple had two daughters, both of whom died before they were four years old. Mrs. McKinley became epileptic and mentally depressed. William took care of her for the rest of his life.

McKinley was elected to the U.S. House from 1876 to 1882 and again from 1886 to 1890. In 1890, he wrote the McKinley tariff, which was popular with wealthy industrialists. McKinley served two terms as governor of Ohio from 1891 to 1895, where he used the National Guard to put down violence in a coal miners' strike, but also raised money to buy food for starving strikers.

The 1896 campaign. In 1896, McKinley was chosen by the Republicans as their presidential candidate. Their platform opposed silver money and favored gold. At the Democratic Convention, William J. Bryan gave his famous "Cross of Gold" speech, opposing gold, and he was chosen as the party's 1896 candidate. Bryan traveled around the country speaking to crowds gathered at railroad stations. McKinley spent his time giving little speeches to crowds who came by train to hear him. Wealthy industrialist Mark Hanna raised money to hire speakers and pay for rallies and campaign advertising for McKinley. McKinley won by 600,000 popular votes, and 271–196 in electoral votes.

McKINLEY AS PRESIDENT. McKinley had a friendly Republican Congress to work with, and he was much smoother with them than Harrison had been. He was able to get higher tariffs passed in 1897 and the Gold Standard Act passed in 1900.

Troubles in Spanish-owned Cuba gained attention after Cubans revolted against Spain in 1895, and American newspapers told how cruelly the Cuban people were treated. Calls for war were fueled by sensational newspaper articles. After the U.S. battleship *Maine* exploded in Havana Harbor on February 15, 1898, and over 250 officers and men were killed, most Americans were convinced the Spanish had done it. The calls for war with Spain increased. McKinley did not favor war but found he was almost alone in opposing it. On April 25, McKinley asked Congress for a declaration of war; Congress approved that day.

The Spanish-American War. The navy was prepared to engage in battle almost immediately. Admiral George Dewey attacked Manila Bay in the Philippines as soon as he could and won an easy victory. A fleet under William Sampson blockaded a Spanish fleet at Santiago Bay in Cuba; when the Spanish tried to escape, they were badly beaten. The U.S. army was small and was built up by state national guards and volunteer units. The most famous of these was Theodore Roosevelt's Rough Riders. Their charge up San Juan Hill thrilled the nation. Spain surrendered in August. The peace treaty gave Cuba, Puerto Rico, Guam, and the Philippines to the United States. Spain received $20 million. The United States gave Cuba independence in 1901.

McKinley easily won reelection in 1900, with Theodore Roosevelt as his vice president. On September 6, 1901, while he was in Buffalo, New York, McKinley was shot by an anarchist, Leon Czolgosz. McKinley died on September 14. Theodore Roosevelt was sworn in as the next president.

Name: _____ Date: _____

Recalling Key Details

Directions: Answer the following questions using what you have learned from the reading selection.

Fact/Opinion:

Write *F* if the statement is a fact or *O* if it is an opinion.

____ 1. Higher tariffs pleased wealthy industrialists.

____ 2. William McKinley favored gold as the backing for U.S. money.

____ 3. Money backed by gold is safer than that backed by silver.

____ 4. The United States had good reasons to go to war with Spain.

____ 5. After the Spanish-American War, the United States gained control of Cuba, Puerto Rico, Guam, and the Philippines.

Multiple Choice:

6. Which job did McKinley never have?
   - A. U.S. senator
   - B. U.S. representative
   - C. Army major
   - D. Governor

7. Who pushed the hardest for war with Spain?
   - A. U.S. senators
   - B. Wealthy industrialists
   - C. Southerners
   - D. Sensationalist newspapers

8. Who had the first victories in the Spanish-American War?
   - A. Spanish navy
   - B. U.S. navy
   - C. U.S. army
   - D. Spanish army

Structured Response:

9. How did Theodore Roosevelt gain fame during the Spanish-American War?

   _____

   _____

   _____

   _____

10. How did McKinley die?

   _____

   _____

   _____

   _____

THEODORE ROOSEVELT
(1858–1919, P. 1901–1909)

Theodore Roosevelt's life was a constant struggle to prove himself. His parents were wealthy and prominent, yet he suffered from poor eyesight and asthma. After he was beaten up by some bullies, Theodore began a vigorous exercise program and took up boxing.

Roosevelt graduated from Harvard in 1880 and married Alice Lee. He tried studying law, but did not like it, so he became a writer. His first book was published in 1882, *The Naval War of 1812*. He was elected to the New York legislature where he served from 1882 to 1884. In 1883, he bought a ranch in the Dakota Territory. It was not financially profitable, but his asthma improved, he mixed with cowboys, and proved himself capable of hardy living.

In 1884, Roosevelt's wife died in childbirth on the same day his mother died. He left his daughter Alice to be cared for by his sister Anna until he later remarried. He retreated for a time to Dakota Territory, pulled himself together, and campaigned for James G. Blaine in the fall. After the election, he returned to writing, and between 1885 and 1889, he wrote seven books. In 1886, he came in third in the mayor's race in New York City. Roosevelt then went to London where he married Edith Carow, whom he had known since childhood. They would go on to have five children. In 1888, he supported Harrison for president, and was given a job as civil service commissioner in 1889. While in that position, he fought political influence in granting jobs and made civil service tests more practical.

The reform mayor of New York City made Roosevelt police commissioner in 1895. Roosevelt put in a merit system for promotions, fought graft, and fired policemen who were not doing their job. This upset the political leaders in the city, and they suggested to President McKinley that he find a good job for Roosevelt in Washington.

In 1897, McKinley appointed him assistant secretary of the navy. Roosevelt was one of those most eager to declare war on Spain. One day, while his boss was out, he sent a message to Admiral Dewey that in case of war with Spain, he was to sail immediately and attack Manila Bay.

When war came, Roosevelt resigned to organize the Rough Riders. He was second in command under Colonel Leonard Wood; when Wood was promoted, Roosevelt was raised to colonel. The Rough Riders were made up of cowboys, some Native Americans, wealthy college graduates, and other eager young men. The Rough Riders were in two battles: Kettle Hill and San Juan Hill. Roosevelt never forgot the men who had served with him. They were friends for life. When he returned from the war, "Teddy" Roosevelt received great attention from the public, as well as from politicians.

Roosevelt ran for governor of New York and won. He began making changes that made him unpopular with New York Republican party leaders such as Tom Platt. They wanted him moved out and suggested that McKinley make Roosevelt his running mate in 1900. At the Republican Convention, Roosevelt was chosen as nominee for vice president by enthusiastic delegates. Roosevelt did the majority of the campaigning with a nation-wide speaking tour.

There was little for Roosevelt to do as vice president. Roosevelt was on a hunting and fishing trip in Vermont when he learned President McKinley was shot. He visited the wounded president, but was assured he would recover, so Roosevelt rejoined his family. When informed that McKinley was dying, Roosevelt returned to Buffalo, but not before McKinley had died. Roosevelt was sworn in as president on September 14, 1901. Now, as one of his critics said: "That cowboy is in the White House."

ROOSEVELT AS PRESIDENT. Unlike Harrison, Cleveland, and McKinley, Theodore Roosevelt left much of the work to his cabinet. He enjoyed playing with his six children and pushed physical exercise for all those around him. White House dinners included a wide variety of guests, from boxers to royalty; all were greeted with equal hospitality. Decisions were made quickly. The public identified with him, and the press loved him. He used the press to get his message across. For the first time, reporters were assigned to the White House to gather news.

Foreign policy was an area where Roosevelt was more free to do things his way than in domestic policy. He wanted the world to see the United States as a major power to be treated with respect. The navy had grown stronger since Chester Arthur had been president, but it had two oceans to patrol. Roosevelt pushed the idea of building a canal across the isthmus between North and South America. Colombia owned Panama in 1903, but the United States and Colombia could not agree on a price for the rights to build a canal there. When the people of Panama revolted against Colombia on November 3, 1903, the United States quickly recognized Panama's independence on November 6 and signed a treaty with Panama for a canal zone. In 1906, Roosevelt went to Panama to see the progress on the canal and by doing that, became the first American president to leave the nation while in office. The Panama Canal opened in 1914 for commercial shipping.

In 1904, war broke out between Russia and Japan, but by 1905, both sides wanted the war to end. Japan asked Roosevelt to work out an agreement between the two sides. Neither side was happy with the treaty, but Roosevelt won the 1906 Nobel Peace Prize for his efforts.

Domestic affairs. While Roosevelt faced many in Congress and in his party who disagreed with him, he easily won the presidential election of 1904. He beat Democrat Alton B. Parker by 336 to 140 electoral votes. Roosevelt was a man of action who wanted things done right away. In this, he was more in line with the thinking of Progressives. They believed that the United States could and should be improved. They wanted clean government, protection of forests, an end to child labor, limits on the hours women worked, limits on alcohol consumption, and improvements in public education.

Roosevelt loved the outdoors and traveled with his friend, Gifford Pinchot, into the woods, often taking his children along. Roosevelt set aside 150 million acres of forest lands for national use. He began to control big business. He enforced the Sherman Antitrust Act, and the Supreme Court broke up a big railroad combination in the Northern Securities Case in 1904. The Pure Food and Drug Act of 1906 began regulation of food and drug sales.

After leaving office, Roosevelt went to Africa on safari and then to Europe. Upon returning, he clashed with President Taft, and in 1912, he ran for president on the Progressive "Bull Moose" ticket. While campaigning in Milwaukee, Wisconsin, on October 14, 1912, he was shot. The bullet traveled through his eyeglasses case and a folded speech before lodging in his chest. He completed his speech before seeking treatment, and the bullet was left in his body for the rest of his life. He later clashed with President Wilson, who would not let him fight in World War I. He died in 1919.

Name: _____ Date: _____

Recalling Key Details

Directions: Answer the following questions using what you have learned from the reading selection.

Matching:

____ 1. Profession Theodore Roosevelt took up after graduating from Harvard

____ 2. Army unit that fought at the Battle of San Juan Hill

____ 3. Where Roosevelt wanted to build a canal across the isthmus between North and South America

____ 4. Where Roosevelt's ranch was

____ 5. Ailment Roosevelt strove to overcome through exercise and living in the west

A. Panama

B. Dakota Territory

C. asthma

D. author

E. Rough Riders

Multiple Choice:

6. How did Roosevelt give out promotions while he was New York City's police commissioner?
   A. He took bribes.
   C. Through a lottery
   B. Through the merit system
   D. Whoever had the most political influence

7. In what position did Roosevelt help prepare the nation for war with Spain?
   A. Assistant secretary of the navy
   C. Governor of New York
   B. Vice president
   D. President

8. Roosevelt won the Nobel Peace Prize in 1906 for negotiating a treaty between which two warring nations?
   A. Colombia and Panama
   C. England and France
   B. Japan and China
   D. Russia and Japan

Structured Response:

9. How did Roosevelt make sure the United States could build a canal across Panama?

   _____

   _____

   _____

10. Which of Roosevelt's actions as president seemed to line up with Progressive reforms?

   _____

   _____

   _____

WILLIAM HOWARD TAFT
(1857–1930, P. 1909–1913)

William Howard Taft was born in Cincinnati, Ohio, in 1857. His father had been secretary of war, attorney general, and an ambassador. William was an excellent student and an above average baseball player. He graduated from Yale in 1878, and received a law degree from Cincinnati Law School in 1880. In 1886, he married Helen Herron. The Tafts had three children. Taft was appointed as a judge of the Ohio superior court and then was named United States solicitor general, the lawyer who argues cases before the U.S. Supreme Court. In 1892, he was appointed as a judge to the U.S. Circuit Court.

President McKinley chose Taft as head of the Philippine Commission, which set up civil government for the Filipinos after the Spanish-American War, and he became the first civil governor of the Philippines. In 1904, he was appointed secretary of war, and he became very close to President Roosevelt.

It took great effort on the part of Roosevelt and Mrs. Taft to convince him to run for president in 1908. The Democrats chose William Jennings Bryan to run for president for the third time. Taft beat him by 1.2 million popular votes and 321–162 in electoral votes.

TAFT AS PRESIDENT. Taft was the heaviest U.S. president, with his weight getting up to 320 pounds at one point. He was often tired, and many times he fell asleep during cabinet meetings. An oversized bathtub was installed in the White House to accommodate him. Taft's main exercise was golf and dancing. In the evening, he and Mrs. Taft danced to phonograph records. He enjoyed baseball games and was known for starting the traditions of throwing out the first ball of the season and the "seventh-inning stretch." The people of Tokyo sent him 3,000 Japanese cherry trees, which were planted along the Potomac River. These are still a major attraction in Washington, D.C.

Taft was not good at politics. He failed to get political or public support for his ideas. Speaker of the House Joe Cannon, an old conservative, stopped any bills he did not like from being considered. When Taft did not support a group of reformers trying to take away some of Cannon's powers, the reformers became angry with him. Taft lost Roosevelt's support after he fired Roosevelt's good friend, Gifford Pinchot, from his position as the chief forester of the United States after a dispute with the secretary of the interior. Although Taft had wanted a lower tariff, the new tariff that was passed was higher than the old one. This made many of the wealthiest Republican Party members angry. Taft also used the Sherman Antitrust Act to break up many large trusts (big businesses controlled by a small number of board members). This further angered wealthy, powerful people.

The 1912 election. In 1912, Taft was tired of being president and only ran to keep Roosevelt from getting the nomination. Roosevelt claimed that Taft had rigged the Republican Convention, so the Roosevelt delegates left the convention and organized the Progressive Party ticket at what was often called the Bull Moose Convention. The Democrats chose Woodrow Wilson, the governor of New Jersey, as their candidate. After Roosevelt was shot in October, all of the candidates stopped campaigning. Wilson easily defeated Roosevelt and Taft, who came in third.

After he left office, Taft was a law school professor and president of the American Bar Association. He served as chairman of the War Labor Board during World War I. In 1921, President Harding appointed him chief justice of the Supreme Court. He was much happier in this role and made the Court much more efficient. He retired from the Court because of bad health in February 1930 and died that March.

Name: _____ Date: _____

Recalling Key Details

Directions: Answer the following questions using what you have learned from the reading selection.

Matching:

_____ 1. The lawyer who argues cases before the U.S. Supreme Court

_____ 2. Convention where the Progressives chose Theodore Roosevelt as their presidential candidate

_____ 3. Sport Taft enjoyed playing as a young man and watching as president

_____ 4. Tradition Taft started

_____ 5. Activity Taft and his wife enjoyed

A. seventh-inning stretch

B. dancing

C. baseball

D. solicitor general

E. Bull Moose

Multiple Choice:

6. What position did Taft have in the new civil government of the Philippines?
   - A. Governor
   - B. President
   - C. Secretary of War
   - D. Chief Justice

7. Who supported Taft for president in 1908 but ran against him in 1912?
   - A. William McKinley
   - B. Woodrow Wilson
   - C. Theodore Roosevelt
   - D. Joe Cannon

8. In what position was Taft the happiest?
   - A. Governor
   - B. President
   - C. Secretary of War
   - D. Chief Justice

Structured Response:

9. Why was Taft not able to get many of his ideas passed by Congress?

   _____

   _____

   _____

   _____

10. How did Roosevelt running as a third candidate affect the election of 1912?

   _____

   _____

   _____

WOODROW WILSON
(1856–1924, P. 1913–1921)

Wilson was born in Virginia, the son of a Presbyterian minister. In 1879, he graduated from Princeton University and then went to the University of Virginia for his law degree. He found practicing law dull and not very profitable. Wilson then studied history and political science at Johns Hopkins University where he earned a Ph.D. He married Ellen Louise Axson in 1885. The couple had three daughters. Wilson was a college professor at Bryn Mawr and Wesleyan, and then he returned to teach at Princeton University in 1890. In 1902, he was named the university's president. He pushed for changes that would make the students more scholarly and the school more democratic.

In 1910, the New Jersey Democrats were looking for a candidate for governor. Wilson resigned as Princeton's president and campaigned hard. He was elected and pushed a number of bills through the legislature to improve local government, reform the election process, and regulate politics and public utilities over the objections of leaders of both political parties. Many reformers from around the country took notice, and a push was made to nominate Wilson for president.

At the Democratic Convention of 1912, Wilson was chosen as the candidate over Speaker of the House Champ Clark. Wilson called for idealism and the "rule of justice and right." His main advantage in the campaign was the wide-open split between Taft and Roosevelt. In the election, Wilson received 435 electoral votes, Roosevelt 88, and Taft 8. In popular votes, his two opponents had over 1 million more popular votes than he had.

WILSON AS PRESIDENT (first term). Wilson was determined to get his New Freedom program through Congress, and he began using an office in the Capitol building to meet with leaders. He called Congress into special session and broke with tradition to appear before a joint session and persuade them to lower the tariff. Part of the new tariff included an income tax, now constitutional under the Sixteenth Amendment.

Wilson next addressed the complex problem of the banking system, and in time, Congress created the Federal Reserve System. The Federal Reserve is the bank from which local banks can borrow money. It controls the rate of interest on loans.

The Clayton Antitrust Act made control over big business stronger. It prohibited unfair business practices. It said that labor unions were not combinations in restraint of trade and that peaceful strikes were legal. The Federal Trade Commission was created to keep an eye on business.

Foreign problems. During a time of revolution in Mexico, Francisco "Poncho" Villa began raiding Mexico and killed 18 Americans at a mining camp. In 1916, Villa captured Columbus, New Mexico, killing 16 Americans. With the new Mexican President Carranza's reluctant permission, Wilson sent General John J. Pershing into Mexico to capture Villa. The search was unsuccessful, and Pershing's men finally returned home in February 1917. This failure gave Germany the impression the U.S. army was weak. During World War I, Germany sent secret agents into Mexico to stir up anger among the Mexican people against the United States.

World War I broke out in Europe in 1914, and one nation after another was drawn in. The Central Powers included Germany, Austria-Hungary, Turkey (the Ottoman Empire), and Bulgaria.

The Allies included Great Britain, France, Russia, and Italy. Wilson issued a Neutrality Proclamation on August 4, 1914, trying to keep the United States out of the war.

Also in August 1914, Ellen Wilson died. However, in 1915, Wilson met the widow, Edith Bolling Galt, and they were married in December.

Neither the Germans nor the British were interested in "playing fair." They both tried to stop any ships from bringing supplies to their enemies. The British started inspecting ships bound for Germany for war supplies, but they did pay for goods taken from ships. German submarine warfare, including the sinking of the British-owned passenger liner *Lusitania* in May 1915 off the Irish coast, brought the United States close to declaring war against Germany. Of the 1,198 people killed, 128 were Americans. Not wanting the United States to enter the war against them, the Germans backed off for a time.

In 1916, the Republicans chose Charles Evans Hughes of the Supreme Court as their presidential candidate. The Democrats chose Wilson again and used the slogan: "He kept us out of the war." Wilson barely won the election, 277–254 in electoral votes.

WILSON AS PRESIDENT (second term). When Germany began "unrestricted submarine warfare," sinking any ship coming close to the British Isles, the United States declared war on Germany in April 1917. Wilson said that it was "a war to end all wars" and was "to make the world safe for democracy."

World War I. By the time the United States entered the war, fighting had been going on in Europe for three years, and the war was not going well for the Allies. They were running out of food, supplies, and soldiers, as the war bogged down in trench warfare. To supply U.S. soldiers and the Allies, the nation's factories were converted to war production and ran at full speed.

To stop the German submarines, the Allies started sending convoys across the Atlantic protected by fast destroyers. The system worked well, and by the end of the war, submarines were far less dangerous for ships than before.

The United States quickly increased the number of its soldiers. By the end of the war, two million had volunteered and two million others had been drafted. The U.S. army sent to fight the war was called the A.E.F. (American Expeditionary Force), and it was led by General John J. Pershing. The first 80,000 American troops arrived in March 1918, and another 663,000 arrived by the end of June. By the fall of 1918, Germans wanted to end the war, but Wilson demanded that their ruler, Kaiser Wilhelm II, resign. After some major battles, the Germans realized they could not win, the Kaiser resigned, and Germany signed an armistice (a temporary agreement to stop fighting) on November 11, 1918. Over 116,000 U.S. soldiers died of wounds or disease, while a total of around 8,500,000 soldiers were killed in World War I. This does not include the civilian deaths.

The peace conference. In January 1918, Wilson announced the Fourteen Points, his goals for the peace treaty. The Fourteenth Point was the creation of a "general association of nations" called the League of Nations to protect the peace in the future. Instead of sending someone to represent him at the Paris Peace Conference, Wilson went to Versailles (the royal estate near Paris) himself to work with other world leaders on the Treaty of Versailles. Germany complained that parts of the treaty were very harsh toward them, but they were forced to sign or face Allied armies invading their country.

The League covenant met strong opposition from Republican Senate leaders, who had not been included in the negotiations. Wilson tried to fight for his League with a speaking tour; however, he suffered a stroke and became paralyzed. After long hearings and debates, the Senate turned down the treaty and the League, but Wilson received the Nobel Peace Prize in 1920 for his efforts. His term as president ended in 1921, and he remained in poor health until his death in 1924.

Name: _____ Date: _____

Recalling Key Details

Directions: Answer the following questions using what you have learned from the reading selection.

Matching:

____	1. University where Woodrow Wilson was president	A.	Princeton
____	2. State where Wilson was governor	B.	labor unions
____	3. The Federal Reserve controls this on loans	C.	submarine
____	4. The Clayton Antitrust Act said that these were not combinations in restraint of trade	D.	New Jersey
		E.	interest
____	5. This type of warfare by the Germans led to the United States declaring war on them in 1917		

Multiple Choice:

6. The failure of the U.S. army to capture Francisco "Pancho" Villa led Germany to try to stir up anger against the United States in what country?
   A. Great Britain   B. Russia
   C. Mexico   D. Cuba

7. The Allies in Europe were running out of supplies and soldiers because the war had stalled due to what style of warfare?
   A. Nuclear   B. Trench
   C. Hand-to-hand   D. Aerial

8. What was the most important part of the Treaty of Versailles for President Wilson?
   A. Making Germany pay for the war   B. Gaining territory from the defeated countries
   C. Providing relief for war refugees   D. Establishing the League of Nations

Structured Response:

9. Why did Germany sign the treaty even though they thought it was unfair?

_____

_____

_____

10. How could the League of Nations have helped countries avoid a future war?

_____

_____

_____

WARREN HARDING
(1865-1923, P. 1921-1923)

Warren Harding was born in Ohio in 1865. His father was a farmer, doctor, and an investor in a newspaper. Young Warren ran errands at the newspaper and worked on his father's farm. He went to Ohio Central College, making average grades. Harding taught for one semester after he left college, but he decided "it was the hardest job I ever had" and quit. His family moved to Marion, Ohio, and he bought a newspaper, the *Marion Star*. Marion was a Republican town in a Democratic county, so even though Harding was a Republican, he had to be careful about how he approached politics.

Harding married Florence Kling DeWolfe, a divorcée with a son, in 1891. Her wealthy father was furious. After they married, Florence started running the newspaper business. She was much better at running the paper than her husband. The Hardings did not have any children together.

In 1898, Harding was elected to the state senate. He met Harry Daugherty, a man wise in politics, who took him up the ladder to success. In 1902, Harding became lieutenant governor. In 1914, he was elected to the U.S. Senate. When a bill came up, he voted the way he thought the people back home wanted and was especially kind to business interests.

In 1920, Harding ran for the Senate again and the presidency at the same time. He did not think he would get the nomination for president, but when none of the favored candidates could get enough delegate votes to win, they turned to Harding. For vice president, the delegates chose Governor Calvin Coolidge of Massachusetts.

The Democrats chose Governor James Cox of Ohio for president and Franklin D. Roosevelt of New York for vice president. Harding won easily because voters blamed the Democrats for the high unemployment, high prices, and wartime government regulations. Despite rumors about Harding's questionable morals, his speeches soothed the voters. He said what America needed was "not heroics but healing, not nostrums [exaggerated cures] but normalcy." Harding beat Cox by seven million popular votes and 404–127 in electoral votes.

HARDING AS PRESIDENT. Some of Harding's advisors were chosen by party leaders: Charles Evans Hughes as secretary of state, Andrew Mellon as secretary of the treasury, and Herbert Hoover as secretary of commerce. Harding also chose former President Taft for the Supreme Court. They did their jobs well, and Harding did not interfere with their work. The Washington Naval Conference, led by Hughes, put limits on the numbers of battleships. Separate treaties with Germany and its allies were negotiated in 1921. Mellon put the government on a budget for the first time and pushed for tax reductions. Hoover encouraged business growth.

Unfortunately, the friends Harding appointed, called the "Ohio gang," took advantage of him. Harry Daugherty was attorney general, and he took bribes. Charles Forbes was in charge of the Veterans Bureau; he and his friends got rich by selling sheets and towels from veterans' hospitals. Harding's poker friend Albert Fall was secretary of the interior. He worked out a scheme to sell oil from government oil reserves set aside for the navy. This was known as the Teapot Dome Scandal. At least two suicides of men involved in the scandals also took place.

As Harding became aware of these abuses, he was sick with worry that all these things would be exposed. He went west for a vacation and died unexpectedly in California on August 2, 1923. After his death, people found out about the scandals, and his memory was disgraced. His death made Calvin Coolidge the next president.

Name: _____ Date: _____

Recalling Key Details

Directions: Answer the following questions using what you have learned from the reading selection.

Matching:

____ 1. Business Warren Harding ran in Marion, Ohio

____ 2. Job that Harding said was the hardest he ever had

____ 3. Harding voted for bills that were kind to these interests

____ 4. Harding said people didn't need nostrums (or exaggerated cures), they needed this

____ 5. Name for the friends Harding appointed in his administration

A. business

B. teaching

C. newspaper

D. Ohio gang

E. normalcy

Multiple Choice:

6. What office did Harding run for at the same time he ran for president?
   A. U.S. representative
   B. U.S. senator
   C. Governor of Ohio
   D. State senator

7. What meeting led to limits being put on the numbers of battleships countries could have?
   A. The Treaty of Versailles
   B. The Ohio Conference
   C. The Washington Naval Conference
   D. The Teapot Dome Debate

8. Who put the government on a budget for the first time?
   A. Andrew Mellon
   B. Charles Evans Hughes
   C. Harry Daugherty
   D. Herbert Hoover

Structured Response:

9. How did Harding's friends take advantage of him and their positions to get rich?

_____

_____

_____

_____

_____

10. Describe Harding's style of governing. How did he deal with issues?

_____

_____

_____

_____

CALVIN COOLIDGE
(1872–1933, P. 1923–1929)

Calvin Coolidge was born in Plymouth, Vermont, a small town where his father ran a country store and was active in local politics. After attending the local school and an academy, Calvin graduated from Amherst College. Coolidge then moved to Massachusetts where he studied law for two years and opened a law practice. He served in many local offices: city council, city attorney, county clerk of the courts, the state legislature, mayor, state senator, lieutenant governor, and governor.

Calvin married Grace Goodhue in 1905; she was outgoing and cheerful; he was shy and serious, but hardworking. They had two sons, one of whom died at age 16 while Calvin was president.

Governor Coolidge gained a reputation beyond Massachusetts during the Boston Police Strike in 1919. When the police commissioner fired 19 policemen who had joined the AFL labor union, the police force went out on strike. When the AFL president protested that some National Guardsmen were used to stop the riots and looting in the city, Coolidge sent him a telegram: "There is no right to strike against the public safety by anybody, anywhere, any time."

At the Republican Convention of 1920, Coolidge was chosen as Harding's vice-presidential running mate. After Harding's landslide victory, the Coolidges moved to Washington and lived in a hotel. President Harding invited Coolidge to sit in on cabinet meetings, but he said little. He presided over the Senate as the Constitution provides, but did not try to draw attention to himself. Whatever rumors and suspicions he heard about Harding, he kept to himself.

Coolidge was on vacation in Vermont when he was notified that President Harding was dead. His father, a notary public, gave him the oath of office as president on August 3, 1923. When he arrived in Washington, the oath was administered again by a Supreme Court justice.

COOLIDGE AS PRESIDENT. Coolidge kept Harding's cabinet without change, but he relied mostly on Herbert Hoover and Andrew Mellon for advice. He had no major policy changes to make in economic matters. He said: "The business of America is business." He didn't want to do anything to interfere with the booming business growth of the 1920s. Coolidge supported reduction of the national debt and cutting government expenses. He opposed sending relief after a terrible flood hit Mississippi until a study of the damage had been finished.

One large industry that did come under regulation was the illegal sale of alcohol in violation of the Eighteenth Amendment and the Volstead Act. Appointed director of the FBI in 1924, J. Edgar Hoover began a crackdown on this business.

Coolidge had not been president long before the rumors about Harding's presidency were being openly discussed. Eventually, former Secretary of the Interior Albert Fall was sentenced to a year in prison for his illegal deals in the Teapot Dome Scandal. Attorney General Harry Daugherty had also received bribes, and he was fired.

The election of 1924. The Democrats were so divided in 1924 they had a hard time picking a candidate. They compromised on John W. Davis, a wealthy New Yorker. Coolidge won 382–136 in electoral votes. Robert LaFollette, the Progressive party candidate, carried only his home state of Wisconsin. The nation was assured another four years of "Coolidge prosperity."

"Silent Cal" was best known for his refusal to use more words than necessary. One woman said she had bet a friend she could get him to say three words, and he answered: "You lose." In 1927, he said: "I do not choose to run for president in 1928."

Name: _____ Date: _____

Recalling Key Details

Directions: Answer the following questions using what you have learned from the reading selection.

Matching:

____ 1. Called out to stop riots and looting during the police strike in Boston

____ 2. State where Calvin Coolidge was born

____ 3. State where Coolidge became governor

____ 4. J. Edgar Hoover cracked down on the illegal sale of this

____ 5. Coolidge supported reducing this

A. Massachusetts
B. Vermont
C. national debt
D. National Guard
E. alcohol

Multiple Choice:

6. Coolidge told the AFL president that no one had a right to strike against what?
   A. The public safety
   B. The state
   C. Unfair working conditions
   D. Low wages

7. Which of these men were punished for their roles in the scandals of President Harding's administration?
   A. Andrew Mellon
   B. Albert Fall
   C. Herbert Hoover
   D. Harry Daugherty

8. The booming economy during the 1920s was often referred to as what?
   A. The 20s boom
   B. Harding's payoff
   C. Coolidge prosperity
   D. Business bonanza

Structured Response:

9. Why did Coolidge not want to interfere with economic matters?

_____

_____

_____

_____

10. Why do you think Coolidge said as little as possible?

_____

_____

_____

HERBERT HOOVER
(1874–1964, P. 1929–1933)

Herbert Hoover was born in West Branch, Iowa, in 1874. His parents died when he was young, and he was taken in by Quaker relatives in Oregon, who taught him the importance of hard work and service. He enrolled in the new Stanford University in California in 1891; it was there that he met Lou Henry. He was an excellent engineering student, and she was a geology student. After graduating, he had engineering jobs in Australia and China. He married Lou in 1898, and the trip to China became their honeymoon. While the Hoovers were there, they were caught up in the Boxer Rebellion and helped organize the foreigners living there for defense against the anti-foreign rioters. Herbert and Lou Hoover had two sons.

Hoover's successful engineering career took him around the world many times. When World War I came, he took charge of relief work in Belgium, and President Wilson appointed him food administrator.

Both political parties wanted him to run on their ticket, but Hoover took the position of secretary of commerce under Presidents Harding and Coolidge. The Commerce Department became the most efficient in the government. In 1928, when it was clear Coolidge did not want another term, Hoover easily won the Republican nomination.

The election of 1928. The Democrats chose as their candidate Governor Al Smith of New York. Smith was Catholic and favored an end to prohibition. Many Americans feared that a Catholic president would let the Pope take over. Hoover did not discuss the religion issue, but he called prohibition a "noble experiment." His party's main theme was prosperity. Hoover won 444–87 in electoral votes and 21.3 million to 15 million in popular votes.

HOOVER AS PRESIDENT. Hoover had been in office six months when the stock market started dropping at alarming rates. On October 29, 1929, the bottom fell out. There were no buyers, and stocks were being sold for practically nothing. Hoover tried to encourage business leaders and gave statements saying that the problem was only temporary and that business would return to normal in weeks. Hoover urged business to increase production and hire more workers; he talked to states about new building projects. Hoover hoped to encourage spending by cutting federal taxes, but the taxes were already so low that it did no good.

Everything began falling apart. People had no money to buy goods, so producers had to lay off workers, and then the unemployed couldn't make their house payments. Banks were in trouble because they had lent money to everyone in this chain. Since their deposits were not insured against bank failure, people started taking their money out, which caused more banks to close.

Hoover did not believe in the federal government giving relief; that was the job of charities and states. He urged farmers to cut crop production and tried lending money to banks, railroads, and other large businesses through the RFC (Reconstruction Finance Corporation). These efforts failed.

The Great Depression had begun, and it was destroying other countries around the world, as well. People began turning to radicals for solutions. In Germany, Hitler came to power, and in Japan, the military replaced the civilian government.

Fair or not, the blame for the Depression fell on Hoover. He was defeated by Democrat Franklin D. Roosevelt in the election of 1932.

Name: _____ Date: _____

Recalling Key Details

Directions: Answer the following questions using what you have learned from the reading selection.

Fact/Opinion:

Write *F* if the statement is a fact or *O* if it is an opinion.

_____ 1. Herbert Hoover was a successful engineer and an efficient government administrator.

_____ 2. Hoover should have tried harder to keep the economy in check.

_____ 3. The federal government should give relief to those who are unemployed or hungry.

_____ 4. Some countries turned to radical leaders to try to solve the problems of the Great Depression.

_____ 5. Banks were unsound institutions and could not be trusted with the people's money.

Multiple Choice:

6. When Hoover and his wife Lou were in China, they were caught up in what event?
   A. The Communist Revolution
   B. World War I
   C. A cholera outbreak
   D. The Boxer Rebellion

7. What happened on October 29, 1929?
   A. Hoover was elected president.
   B. The stock market crashed.
   C. World War II began.
   D. The Boxer Rebellion began.

8. What job did Hoover never have?
   A. Secretary of Commerce
   B. Engineer
   C. Vice President
   D. Food administrator

Structured Response:

9. What were some of the measures Hoover took to try to help the economy?

_____

_____

_____

_____

_____

10. If you were a farmer who had bills and loans to pay, what would happen if you cut crop production?

_____

_____

_____

FRANKLIN D. ROOSEVELT
(1882–1945, P. 1933–1945)

Franklin Roosevelt, or FDR as he came to be called later, was born into a wealthy family residing at Hyde Park, New York. His fifth cousin, Theodore Roosevelt, was a Republican, but he was close to Franklin's father, James, a loyal Democrat. Franklin attended Groton Academy. In 1900, he entered Harvard. He was only an average student but earned his degree in three years. While at Harvard, he fell in love with Eleanor Roosevelt, a distant cousin, who was Theodore's niece. After graduating from Harvard, he married Eleanor in 1905. After a year at Columbia University Law School, he became a lawyer.

Eleanor was an unusual person. She was born into a wealthy family, but she never cared much for wealth or position. She had been very shy as a girl, but Eleanor changed over the years into a dynamic woman with the ability to meet a world leader as well as a common person and to make both feel welcome. By the end of her life, people were calling her "First Lady of the World." She and Franklin were the parents of six children.

In 1910, Franklin was elected to the state senate. He was involved in several presidential campaigns: in 1912, he campaigned for Woodrow Wilson; in 1920, he ran with James M. Cox as the vice-presidential candidate; in 1924 and 1928, he campaigned for Al Smith. He was assistant secretary of the navy in the Wilson administration, where he learned much about national defense and foreign policy.

In 1921, Roosevelt contracted polio; his legs were paralyzed, and he was in great pain. By hard work and determination, he was able to walk again within a year with the aid of heavy braces. He built up his upper body to compensate for the weakness of his lower body. He began going down to Warm Springs, Georgia, to swim and strengthen his legs. Eleanor kept him involved in politics and his law career. His appearance at the 1924 Democratic convention slowly walking across the stage brought him a standing ovation from the crowd.

FDR was elected governor of New York in 1928. The state was hard hit by the Depression, and FDR pushed a number of programs to help the poor and unemployed. To pay for the programs, income taxes were raised on the wealthy.

After receiving the nomination at the 1932 Democratic Convention, FDR flew to Chicago to address the convention, the first time that had been done by any presidential candidate. He told them: "I pledge you, I pledge myself, to a new deal for the American people." The name "New Deal" stuck.

The campaign of 1932. FDR loved to campaign and gave 16 major speeches, each devoted to one topic. Herbert Hoover argued that the Depression had been caused by worldwide collapse, and Democrats in Congress had refused to cooperate with him in finding answers. When the people voted, FDR won by over seven million popular votes and 472–59 in electoral votes. It was clear that the nation wanted a new deal.

ROOSEVELT AS PRESIDENT (first term). By March 1933, when FDR became president, one of every four Americans was unemployed, 5,504 banks had closed, and many farmers were losing their land because they could not pay their mortgages. Veterans who had marched on Washington demanding their pensions immediately had been driven out of town by soldiers with tanks. FDR assured the nation in his inaugural address that "The only thing we have to fear is fear itself." Congress quickly approved FDR's new programs in what came to be known as the "Hundred Days."

FDR began with the banking crisis. All banks were closed until their books could be examined to decide which were strong enough to survive. FDR went on the radio with his first "Fireside Chat" to assure people that when their bank reopened, their money would be safe. The people believed him, and more deposited their money than withdrew it. The Federal Deposit Insurance Corporation (FDIC) was created to insure banks.

To save money, FDR cut the salaries of federal workers and veterans' pensions. Another group of veterans came to Washington. Instead of driving them out, he sent hot coffee to them and had some of the veterans meet with one of his assistants, and then they all went home.

New spending programs came one after another. The Civilian Conservation Corps (CCC) was created to employ young men in work projects. The Federal Emergency Relief Administration (FERA) gave states money for relief programs. The Agricultural Adjustment Act was created to pay farmers to take land out of production. The National Recovery Administration (NRA) called for meetings of industries to set prices. All manufacturers had to charge the same price for the same products. All wages for certain types of workers were the same across the industry, as well. The labor codes abolished child labor. The Tennessee Valley Authority (TVA) was created to build dams along the Tennessee River for flood control and to provide electric power. However, thousands of people in that area had to sell their homes and land and move because they would soon be under water. In 1934, the Securities and Exchange Commission (SEC) was created to correct problems in the stock market. The Federal Communications Commission (FCC) regulated the communications industry: radio stations, telephone, and telegraph.

Government was now regulating economic areas it had never touched before, and while FDR remained popular, there were critics who did not like what was happening. The rich were unhappy with the new taxes and regulations, but there were others who called for even heavier taxes on the wealthy and for programs to help the elderly.

The Supreme Court was also critical of some New Deal programs. The Court declared the NRA unconstitutional in 1935. Part of the AAA was ruled unconstitutional in 1936, and a second AAA was created to avoid the mistakes of the first one. FDR was angry with the Court for its criticism, and he referred to the Court as "the nine old men."

FDR felt the pressure for even more changes. The Works Progress Administration (WPA) was created to give jobs to all kinds of people, from the very skilled to the unskilled. Most of its money went to street and road projects, public buildings, and parks. The Rural Electrification Administration (REA) brought electric power to rural areas. Social Security came in 1935 as an insurance program to help those over 65 years of age, the blind, and crippled children.

The election of 1936. By 1936, few Republicans held any high offices. They were outnumbered in the House 103 to 319 and in the Senate 25 to 69. The Republican candidate for president was Governor Alf Landon of Kansas. Roosevelt won 523–8 in the electoral vote and by over 11 million popular votes. The new Congress was even more Democratic.

The Supreme Court battle. FDR was feeling confident, and he now made one of the few serious political mistakes of his career. He planned to add up to six more members to the Supreme Court. It took little time for Congress and the public to react against the president. FDR's proposal went down in flaming defeat in Congress. Within months, two Supreme Court justices retired and two died; the whole fight had been unnecessary. Roosevelt could now appoint justices more favorable to his policies.

There was a rise in unemployment in 1937, and a new agency, the Public Works Administration (PWA), began new building projects in nearly every U.S. county. By 1939, it had spent $6 billion.

By 1938, FDR had more critics than ever before, and the public elected 79 more Republicans to the House and eight to the Senate. Southern Democrats in Congress even joined with Republicans to block his more liberal programs. The New Deal period had ended.

The election of 1940. Had it not been for a new world crisis, the story of FDR might have ended in 1940, but the new war threat extended his administration. FDR ran for a third term against Republican Wendell Willkie of Indiana, and a nation that felt it needed experience rather than change voted for him.

World War II. Dictatorships, communist nations, and Fascists began to dominate Europe and Asia in the 1930s. Americans began to worry that another war was imminent.

In 1935, a series of actions took place as dictators began grabbing land. The Germans, led by Adolf Hitler, and the Italians, led by Benito Mussolini, began expanding their territories. The Spanish Civil War began in 1936, with Germany helping one side and the Russians helping the other. The Japanese started bombing Shanghai, China, in 1937. In 1938, Germany took Austria and the Sudeten land from Czechoslovakia. In March of 1939, Germany took the rest of Czechoslovakia and invaded Poland on September 1. On September 3, Great Britain and France declared war on Germany. World War II had begun. In 1940, Hitler attacked Norway, Denmark, Holland, and France. In September 1941, Germany attacked the Soviet Union in an effort to reach its oil fields in the Crimea. The attack was slowed by rain, then snow.

Americans wanted to stay out of the war, but they also wanted to build up U.S. defenses and support their allies. The United States began a "cash and carry" policy; if a nation at war wanted supplies, it could pay for them and carry them home in their own ships. By September 1940, the U.S. defense budget had reached $13 billion, and taxes were raised. The first peacetime draft came in 1940, and about 800,000 men were drafted in one year. State National Guards had also been called into active service. The United States sent 50 old destroyers to England to protect convoys crossing the Atlantic. The lend-lease program began in 1941 to send supplies to friendly nations at war. They also sent supplies to China.

The United States enters the War. On December 7, 1941, without warning, the Japanese attacked the U.S. naval and air bases in and near Pearl Harbor in Hawaii, killing 2,335 military personnel and wounding over 1,000. The next day, the United States declared war on Japan, and on December 11, the United States declared war on Germany and Italy.

The war years were very busy for the Roosevelts. Mrs. Roosevelt traveled to military bases and sent reports to FDR. In 1941, FDR addressed the nation in what is known as the Four Freedoms Speech. He considered these freedoms essential for world peace: freedom of speech, freedom of religion, freedom from want, and freedom from fear. He made the speech to encourage Americans to support those who were fighting in Word War II.

In 1942, 26 Allied countries signed the Atlantic Charter, agreeing to fight until victory could be won over the Axis powers. FDR suggested the group call themselves the "United Nations." This was the beginning of the United Nations organization formed at the end of the war.

The election of 1944. FDR and his new vice-presidential running mate Harry S Truman easily beat the Republican candidate Thomas Dewey. While FDR did appear tired and run down, Americans were not about to change leadership in the middle of the war.

The president traveled secretly to meetings of Allied leaders in Casablanca, Cairo, and Yalta. The trip to Yalta in February 1945 was the most demanding for FDR. Josef Stalin, the Russian leader, was difficult to deal with. The president reported back to Congress when he returned from Yalta and then went to Warm Springs, Georgia, to rest. He died April 12, 1945, weeks before the war against Germany ended and four months before Japan's surrender.

Name: _____ Date: _____

Recalling Key Details

Directions: Answer the following questions using what you have learned from the reading selection.

Matching:

_____ 1. Disease caused by a virus that can cause fever, paralysis, deterioration of muscles, and even death

_____ 2. The name of Franklin D. Roosevelt's economic program during the Great Depression

_____ 3. FDR's radio addresses that helped inform and calm people

_____ 4. If a nation at war bought supplies from the United States, they could transport them home on their own ships.

_____ 5. An agreement among Allied countries to fight until the Axis powers were defeated

A. cash and carry
B. New Deal
C. Atlantic Charter
D. polio
E. Fireside Chats

Multiple Choice:

6. Where did the money come from to pay for many of FDR's new relief programs?
   A. High tariffs
   B. Taxes on the wealthy
   C. Taxes on the working class
   D. Loans from foreign countries

7. Which program built dams for flood protection and to provide electric power in the south?
   A. National Recovery Administration
   B. Federal Emergency Relief Administration
   C. Tennessee Valley Authority
   D. Civilian Conservation Corps

8. Who attacked the U.S. naval base at Pearl Harbor, causing the United States to enter World War II?
   A. The Japanese
   B. The Germans
   C. The Russians
   D. The Italians

Structured Response:

9. How did Eleanor Roosevelt help her husband with his career?

_____

_____

_____

10. What events helped FDR get reelected when voters might have normally tired of him?

_____

_____

_____

HARRY S TRUMAN
(1884–1972, P. 1945–1953)

Harry Truman was born in Lamar, Missouri, in 1884, and his family moved to Independence, Missouri, when he was six years old. As a boy, his poor eyesight and thick glasses made it impossible for him to play sports, so he read instead, especially history. He dreamed of going to West Point, but his poor eyesight kept him out. His family did not have enough money for him to attend college. After working in the Kansas City area, he returned to the farm. In August 1917, he was sent with his National Guard unit to France as a first lieutenant. His unit, Battery D, was in some of the worst fighting. He left the army as a captain. He married Bess Wallace, his childhood girlfriend, seven weeks after returning from the war. They had one daughter, Margaret. Truman and a partner opened a men's clothing store in Kansas City, but the hard times of 1921–1922 forced the store to close.

One of the men he had met in France introduced Truman to his uncle, Boss Tom Pendergast, who ran politics in Kansas City and Jackson County, Missouri. With Pendergast's help, Truman was elected a county judge (commissioner) and proved more honest and independent than anyone could have imagined. He was elected to the Senate in 1934, where he supported New Deal programs. After he was reelected in 1940, the Truman Committee was created to watch for waste and corruption in the building of military camps, and it saved taxpayers billions of dollars.

In 1944, President Franklin Roosevelt was pressured into choosing a new running mate. Truman was chosen although he had made no effort to get the job. His vice presidency lasted 82 days. FDR died on April 12, 1945, and Truman was sworn in as president by the chief justice of the Supreme Court. Few believed Truman was up to the tasks ahead. He had neither the formal education nor the background in international affairs most felt was needed for the job. FDR had not told him about many of the problems the world and nation faced.

TRUMAN AS PRESIDENT (first term). Events were moving at lightning speed, and Truman reacted quickly to them. The war was coming to an end, and the meeting to form the United Nations was to be held on April 25. Germany surrendered on May 7, 1945, and Truman met at Potsdam, Germany, with Stalin and Churchill in July. Big issues faced the leaders as to what would happen to the small nations of Eastern Europe. Little was accomplished because Stalin wanted to make the region communist.

Truman was not told about the atomic bomb project, code-named the Manhattan Project, until after he became president. He appointed a committee to study the moral and military issues involved in using the bomb, but he made the final decision to use the bombs. He felt the lives saved by ending the war quickly justified the use of the devastating bombs. Atomic bombs were dropped on Hiroshima, Japan, on August 6, and on Nagasaki, Japan, on August 9; Japan surrendered on August 14, 1945.

The end of World War II was the beginning of Truman's struggles with Congress. He proposed a number of New Deal-type programs including federal aid to education, an increase in the minimum wage, medical insurance, and civil rights laws. He wanted to continue the Office of Price Administration (OPA) that had kept prices under control during the war. When the OPA controls ended in 1946, prices rose faster than wages.

Labor unions began striking for higher wages, the most critical being strikes by the coal miners and railway unions. Truman threatened to draft striking railway workers into the army and make them run the trains; the strike ended before he could carry out the threat. Coal miners ignored a court order not to strike. The union was fined $3.5 million, and its leader, John L. Lewis, was personally fined $10,000. Lewis finally gave in and ended the strike, but Truman's handling of the situation made him unpopular with unions.

In the 1946 elections, Republicans gained control of both Houses of Congress. They passed the Taft-Hartley Labor Law, which said a person did not have to join a union to work, permitted employers to sue unions for breach of contract, and required a 60-day waiting period before a strike could take place. The law passed over Truman's veto.

Truman was able to get Congress to work with him on world problems. He gained Republican support for programs to stop Communist expansion. The most important of these were the Truman Doctrine, which promoted supporting free people to resist the spread of Communism by providing aid to Greece and Turkey, and the Marshall Plan to rebuild Europe's economy.

The defense of the United States was changed by three actions. The War and Navy Departments were combined to form the Department of Defense. To gather information on other nations, the Central Intelligence Agency (CIA) was formed. To give the president a better view of the world, the National Security Council (NSC) was created.

The election of 1948. Truman was chosen by the Democrats as their presidential nominee, but not without bitter arguments. Southern Democrats walked out of the convention to protest Truman's civil rights program, and they formed the States' Rights Democratic Party (Dixiecrats) led by Strom Thurmond. The Henry Wallace faction of the party blamed Truman for the troubles with the Soviet Union; they left to form the Progressive Party. The Republicans confidently chose Governor Thomas E. Dewey of New York as their candidate.

Truman blasted Congress for the nation's troubles in a railroad "whistle stop" campaign. Dewey avoided the tough issues in carefully worded speeches. Even though Truman was far behind in the polls, his efforts paid off. The electoral vote was Truman 303, Dewey 189, and Thurmond 39. The election also put Democrats in control of both Houses of Congress.

TRUMAN AS PRESIDENT (second term). Much of Truman's time during the second term was devoted to foreign problems. The Soviet Union was expanding its control in Europe. West Berlin was like a small island in a Communist sea. In 1948, the city was cut off from the road and railroad bridge that had been its supply line across East Germany. The airlift authorized by Truman brought planes carrying supplies into the airports of West Berlin every two to three minutes. By 1949, the Soviets realized that they had lost and lifted the blockade. The non-Communist nation of West Germany was formed in 1949.

The Communist Chinese advanced across that nation, and they drove the Nationalists out of China. The pro-American Nationalists set up their government in Formosa (Taiwan).

The North Atlantic Treaty Organization (NATO) was formed in 1949, and in 1950, General Eisenhower was named its commander. While most American attention was on Europe, war broke out in Korea.

North Korea attacked South Korea, an American ally, in June 1950. Truman acted quickly and sent troops and airplanes to help South Korea. The North Koreans pushed the American and South Korean armies into a small area on the east coast. General Douglas MacArthur then surprised the North Koreans by an attack on the west coast at Inchon. With more help coming, the North Koreans were pushed back north near China. MacArthur wanted to expand the war, and he violated Truman's orders to limit the war. Finally, Truman fired him. The war reached a stalemate, and peace talks were held, but an armistice was not signed until July 27, 1953, after Truman had left office.

Name: _____ Date: _____

Recalling Key Details

Directions: Answer the following questions using what you have learned from the reading selection.

Matching:

_____ 1. Location where Truman met with Stalin and Churchill

_____ 2. City devastated by the first atomic bomb

_____ 3. Southern Democrats who walked out of the 1948 convention to protest Truman's civil rights program

_____ 4. Where the Chinese Nationalists set up their government

_____ 5. Location of an airlift to bring supplies into a city cut off by a Communist blockade

A. Dixiecrats

B. Taiwan

C. Hiroshima

D. Potsdam

E. West Berlin

Multiple Choice:

6. What type of striking workers did Harry Truman threaten to draft into the army?
   - A. Coal miners
   - B. Railway workers
   - C. Police
   - D. Pilots

7. Which program helped rebuild Europe after World War II?
   - A. Office of Price Administration
   - B. United Nations
   - C. North Atlantic Treaty Organization
   - D. Marshall Plan

8. What country was Truman helping when he sent troops and planes in 1950?
   - A. North Korea
   - B. South Korea
   - C. West German
   - D. Turkey

Structured Response:

9. How did Truman try to control labor unions?

   _____

   _____

   _____

   _____

10. How was the Truman Doctrine supposed to stop the spread of Communism?

   _____

   _____

   _____

   _____

DWIGHT EISENHOWER
(1890–1969, P. 1953–1961)

Dwight Eisenhower was born in Texas but was raised in Abilene, Kansas. His father was a mechanic at a creamery. Eisenhower graduated from West Point in 1915. He was then stationed in Texas, where he met Mamie Doud, whom he married in 1916. The Eisenhowers had two sons, one of whom died as a child.

Most of Eisenhower's early jobs in the army entailed being an assistant to others with higher rank. He worked for the assistant secretary of war; he then went to the Philippines as an assistant to General Douglas MacArthur. In 1940, he was named chief of staff of the Third Division. Then in 1941, General George Marshall picked him to be his assistant.

By 1942, Eisenhower was the commanding general of the European Theater of Operation in World War II. He was given the job of leading the invasion of North Africa, then Sicily and Italy. Most important of all, he was named the supreme commander of allied forces and was in charge of the invasion of Normandy on D-Day. He led his men to victory over Germany. After the war, Eisenhower was named army chief of staff and was in charge of cutting the size of the army.

In 1948, Eisenhower published a book, *Crusade in Europe,* and served as president of Columbia University for two years. In 1950, he was picked to lead NATO by President Truman. With the war in Korea going badly, both parties wanted Eisenhower as their presidential nominee in the 1952 election. Eisenhower decided he was a Republican.

The election of 1952. The Democrats chose Governor Adlai Stevenson of Illinois as their candidate. The Republican mottoes were: "It's time for a change" and "I like Ike." (Ike was Eisenhower's nickname.) Eisenhower carried all but nine states, and he won the election 442–89 in electoral votes. For the first time since 1933, a Republican was living in the White House.

EISENHOWER AS PRESIDENT (first term). Eisenhower appointed business leaders to most jobs in his administration. Each was responsible for running his or her department and was required to send reports to him on what was happening. Whenever anything went wrong, it was the cabinet member, not Eisenhower, whom the public blamed. The key people around the president were John Foster Dulles, secretary of state; Charles Wilson, secretary of defense; and Sherman Adams, his chief of staff. Many problems arose during his first term in office.

The most pressing problem was ending the war in Korea. Eisenhower fulfilled a campaign promise by going to Korea and meeting officers and enlisted men there. The peace talks came to an end after months of arguing. The new line between North and South Korea was very close to where it was when the war started, wavering along or near the 38th parallel.

At home, Senator Joe McCarthy conducted hearings into charges that Communists had snuck into high positions. Many in government and the movie industry were ruined by being accused of being Communists. Eisenhower said he didn't want to get into the gutter with McCarthy. However, after McCarthy accused the army of hiding Communists, a new set of hearings attacked McCarthy himself. He was censured (officially criticized) by the Senate in 1954; he died in 1957.

One of Eisenhower's first appointees was Earl Warren as chief justice of the Supreme Court. In 1954, the Supreme Court handed down the *Brown v. Topeka Board of Education* decision, which said segregation in education violated the 14th Amendment of the Constitution. Some states began allowing African-American and white students to attend school together, but others refused, which led to trouble in southern schools for years to come.

In 1956, the Supreme Court also ruled that segregation on buses was illegal after Rosa Parks, an African-American woman, refused to give up her seat to a white man on a bus in Montgomery, Alabama. She was arrested, and African Americans refused to ride city buses until they were treated more fairly. The leader of the bus boycott was Dr. Martin Luther King, Jr.

Other significant issues were addressed. Taxes were cut, more people were made eligible for Social Security, student loans were given to college students, and the building of interstate highways began.

Two serious international problems occurred simultaneously. Egypt decided to take over the Suez Canal, which was owned by British and French investors. The United States was disturbed when paratroopers were sent to the Canal by the British and French governments. At the same time, the Soviets sent troops into Hungary to put down a revolt against the unpopular Communist government.

Eisenhower suffered a major heart attack in 1956 but was recovering by the time of the election. In 1956, he easily defeated Adlai Stevenson again.

EISENHOWER AS PRESIDENT (second term). The most serious problem at home was ending segregation of schools in some southern states. Eisenhower did not approve of segregating students, but he thought a gradual approach was best. On the other hand, he knew the Constitution had to be enforced. In 1957, he had to federalize 10,000 Arkansas National Guardsmen and then send in 1,000 paratroopers to keep order when riots broke out over letting African-American students attend Little Rock, Arkansas', Central High School. Progress was very slow, and stubborn opposition caused trouble in many places in the South. When Eisenhower left office, there were still no African Americans attending school with whites in four states, and less than two percent attended with whites in seven others.

Foreign affairs. The most dangerous situation for all Americans was the Cold War with the Soviet Union. The threat of a war using atomic and hydrogen weapons terrified some people so much they built bomb shelters and stocked them with food and water.

In 1957, the Soviets launched the world's first man-made satellite, *Sputnik I.* The United States was stunned. The following year, NASA was formed to begin a strong U.S. space program, and the federal government put money into school science programs.

The Soviets felt they had the upper hand now, and they told the West it must give up Berlin in six months or the Soviets would turn it over to the East Germans. The NATO members joined together and made it clear they were not going to turn over Berlin. The Soviet leader, Nikita Khruschev, realized they meant business and started a public relations effort to show that the Soviet Union was a peaceful nation. Khruschev came to the United States and other western nations to show his good intentions. However, just before a summit meeting of world leaders in Paris in 1960, an American U-2 spy plane was shot down 1,200 miles inside Soviet territory. Eisenhower said he knew about the flight, and Khruschev broke up the summit.

A new problem was developing closer to home. The Communist Fidel Castro took over in Cuba, and he let the United States know he was going to take over U.S.-owned businesses in Cuba. Eisenhower allowed Cuban refugees to be trained to overthrow Castro.

Eisenhower remained popular to the end of his time in office, and the United States remained strong and prosperous. He retired to his farm near Gettysburg, Pennsylvania, and wrote the memoirs of his years as president. He died on March 28, 1969.

Name: _____ Date: _____

Recalling Key Details

Directions: Answer the following questions using what you have learned from the reading selection.

Matching:

____ 1. Where the D-Day invasion took place

____ 2. Dividing line between North and South Korea

____ 3. Senator McCarthy accused people of being this

____ 4. Trouble in the south centered around this

____ 5. This type of plane was shot down inside Soviet territory

A. segregation

B. U-2

C. 38th parallel

D. Communists

E. Normandy

Multiple Choice:

6. Which country took over the Suez Canal from British and French investors?
    A. The Soviet Union
    C. Turkey
    B. Israel
    D. Egypt

7. The United States pushed for a stronger space program after what nation launched *Sputnik I*?
    A. The Soviet Union
    C. China
    B. Egypt
    D. Cuba

8. Which country close to the United States was taken over by a Communist leader?
    A. Egypt
    C. Cuba
    B. Turkey
    D. The Soviet Union

Structured Response:

9. How did the Supreme Court start to end segregation in the south?

_____

_____

_____

_____

_____

10. Why did Eisenhower not get blamed many times when things went wrong during his administration?

_____

_____

_____

_____

JOHN F. KENNEDY
(1917–1963, P. 1961–1963)

John Fitzgerald Kennedy was born on May 29, 1917, in Brookline, Massachusetts, to a life in politics. On his mother's side, his grandfather had been mayor of Boston and served in the U.S. House. His father, Joseph, was very active in politics as well as business, and he had been appointed to head the Securities and Exchange Commission by President Roosevelt; Joseph Kennedy was later named ambassador to Great Britain. All the Kennedy sons were groomed to become successful in politics. Their names were Joe Jr.; John; Robert; and Edward (Ted).

John Kennedy graduated from Harvard in 1940. His senior thesis, *Why England Slept,* indicated his belief that weakness produces a dangerous foreign policy.

During World War II, Joe Jr., was killed in a bombing run over Germany. John had volunteered for the navy and was given command of PT-109, a patrol torpedo boat. It was rammed by a Japanese destroyer. Even though he was badly injured, John towed a crew member five hours to an island, using a strap he held in his mouth. The crew was rescued four days later, and after his recovery in the hospital, Kennedy was discharged with a Navy and Marine Corps Medal.

In 1946, Kennedy ran for the U.S. House from a Boston district and easily won. In 1952, he was elected to the Senate by a small margin. He married Jacqueline Bouvier in 1953. In 1956, he tried for the vice presidential nomination but was defeated. While he was recovering from a spinal operation in 1956, he wrote *Profiles in Courage,* which won the Pulitzer Prize.

The election of 1960. In 1960, Kennedy gained the Democratic nomination for president and chose Lyndon Johnson, Senate majority leader from Texas, as his vice presidential running mate. His Republican opponent was Vice President Richard Nixon. Although Nixon did not personally use the religion issue, many Protestants feared a Catholic would follow orders from the Pope. Kennedy said his duty was to the nation, not to the church. During the campaign, Kennedy debated Nixon in the first televised presidential debate. Kennedy seemed more impressive than Nixon to many people. When the votes were counted, Kennedy had barely won 303–219 in electoral votes.

KENNEDY AS PRESIDENT. In his inaugural address, Kennedy challenged the nation and world to "ask not what your country can do for you—ask what you can do for your country." Kennedy aroused enthusiasm for public service among many young people. He established the Peace Corps volunteer service organization by executive order in 1961. Those around him shared his enthusiasm for getting things done. Among these "New Frontiersmen" as they were called were Robert MacNamara (secretary of defense), Douglas Dillon (a Republican and secretary of the treasury), Dean Rusk (secretary of state), and Kennedy's brother, Robert (attorney general). The public was enchanted with Kennedy's family, often referring to this time as "Camelot," and they took countless pictures of his wife, Jacqueline, and their children, Caroline and John Jr.

Civil rights. The most troubling domestic issue of the time was civil rights. The most prominent civil rights leader was Dr. Martin Luther King, Jr. His approach was peaceful, but firm. If any violence occurred during a demonstration, it would be by the opponent. The NAACP, the oldest civil rights group, was very effective in courts, winning cases against discrimination. A new group, the Congress of Racial Equality (CORE) used sit-ins and other means to break segregation in bus transportation and at lunch counters.

At first, Kennedy was reluctant to tangle with the southern Democrats in Congress, but where he could act, he did. He increased the numbers of African Americans in better government jobs. When CORE "freedom riders" were attacked by mobs at bus depots, 600 deputy U.S. marshals were sent to restore order. The Interstate Commerce Commission ordered segregation ended in terminals.

When the governor of Mississippi refused to admit James Meredith, a well-qualified Air Force veteran, to the University of Mississippi, Robert Kennedy obtained a court order forbidding the governor to interfere. The governor ignored the order. When Meredith arrived on the campus with federal marshals, they were attacked by a mob. President Kennedy federalized the National Guard and order was restored; but by that time, two had been killed and hundreds were injured.

In Birmingham, Alabama, civil rights workers led by Dr. King tangled with crowds at stores and restaurants that refused to serve African Americans. Police Commissioner "Bull" Connor used clubs, police dogs, and fire hoses to stop street demonstrations. When Governor George Wallace personally blocked African Americans from entering the University of Alabama, Kennedy federalized the Alabama National Guard and forced Wallace to back down. Kennedy asked Congress for stronger civil rights laws. Civil rights leaders organized the March on Washington, which brought 250,000 to a dramatic rally at the Lincoln Memorial.

Foreign policy. Cuba gave Kennedy his greatest embarrassment as well as his greatest victory in a test of wills with Fidel Castro and Nikita Khruschev. When Kennedy learned that Cuban refugees had been trained for an invasion of communist Cuba by the CIA, he gave the green light for the invasion. The Bay of Pigs invasion began April 17, 1961, but 1,000 of the invaders were captured. The invasion was a complete failure.

Khruschev, the Soviet Union's leader, thinking the United States was in weak hands, again threatened to turn West Berlin over to East Germany. Kennedy did not budge on this issue, and asked Congress for the power to call up reserves. He then increased the number of draftees and told the United States: "We seek peace, but we shall not surrender." Instead of merely threatening, the Soviets built a wall around West Berlin, preventing anyone from East Germany from immigrating to West Berlin. Kennedy sent 1,500 more troops into Berlin. The Soviets backed off, and the crisis passed.

The Cold War reached a climax during the Cuban Missile Crisis when in 1962, the Soviet Union planned to put nuclear weapons on missiles based in Cuba. The missiles had a range of up to 2,000 miles, which could easily reach many of the major cities in the United States. The United States put a blockade around Cuba and threatened to search any ship within a zone around the island. The tension grew as Soviet ships carrying missiles came close to the blockade, but at the last minute, they were ordered to return home. To help prevent future crises, a "hot line" was installed that summer between the White House and the Kremlin.

War in Vietnam continued despite a dividing line having been drawn between North and South Vietnam in 1954. The pro-American South Vietnamese government was unpopular with the public there. Kennedy sent well-trained troops, the Green Berets, to train the South Vietnamese army how to fight more effectively.

On November 22, 1963, while in an open car in a motorcade in Dallas, Texas, the president was shot by a gunman from the window of a six-story building. Kennedy was rushed to the hospital, and he died minutes later. His body was flown to Washington as a stunned nation watched. The gunman, Lee Harvey Oswald, was captured. However on November 24, as he was being transferred from one jail to another, he was shot and killed by nightclub operator Jack Ruby. Kennedy is buried in Arlington National Cemetery.

Name: _____ Date: _____

Recalling Key Details

Directions: Answer the following questions using what you have learned from the reading selection.

Matching:

____ 1. Failed invasion of Cuba

____ 2. Civil rights group that was effective at winning cases against discrimination

____ 3. Civil rights group that used sit-ins to break segregation in bus transportation and at lunch counters

____ 4. The Soviets built a wall around this city that was surrounded by East Germany

____ 5. A means of communication installed between the White House and the Kremlin

A. West Berlin

B. Bay of Pigs

C. hot line

D. NAACP

E. CORE

Multiple Choice:

6. In which states did President John Kennedy federalize the National Guard to protect African-American students?

   A. Florida   B. Alabama

   C. Texas   D. Mississippi

7. The blockade around Cuba was to keep what out?

   A. Cuban refugees   B. Food and supplies

   C. Soviet missiles with nuclear warheads   D. Counterfeit goods made in Cuba

8. Who assassinated President Kennedy?

   A. Jack Ruby   B. George Wallace

   C. Robert MacNamara   D. Lee Harvey Oswald

Structured Response:

9. How was the United States involved in the Vietnam War during Kennedy's administration?

   _____

   _____

   _____

10. In what instances did Kennedy remain firm and get the Soviets to back down?

   _____

   _____

   _____

LYNDON B. JOHNSON
(1908–1973, P. 1963–1969)

Lyndon Johnson grew up in a very political family, who lived in the sandhills of southwest Texas and valued hard work. As a boy, he did various odd jobs, from picking cotton and shining shoes to waiting tables and washing dishes. He graduated from Southwest Texas State Teachers College in 1930 and taught for a while. He worked hard for the "Kleberg for Congress" campaign; when Kleberg won, he took Johnson to Washington as his secretary. In 1934, Johnson married Claudia (nicknamed Lady Bird) Taylor, whose father was a wealthy oil man. The Johnsons had two daughters. In 1935, he went back to Texas to lead the National Youth Administration (NYA), working to find jobs for college students.

In 1937, Johnson was elected to the U.S. House, where he was a good "New Dealer" and became popular with Franklin Roosevelt. He was soon known as a man who got things done for his district and his state. In 1941, he was given special leave by the House to go into active service in the Navy Reserve and was commissioned as lieutenant commander. In 1942, he received the Silver Star for gallantry under fire. After FDR ordered all members of Congress serving in the armed forces to return home, his active career in the navy ended, but he continued in the Naval Reserves.

In 1948, Johnson was elected senator from Texas and was named to the Armed Services Committee. He was often critical of Truman's conduct during the Korean War.

Unlike some Democrats, he cooperated with Eisenhower's Republican administration. In 1953, he was elected Senate minority leader, and after the 1954 election, he became majority leader. In 1957, he was active in getting the civil rights bill passed that Eisenhower had asked for. He favored a larger air force after the Soviets launched *Sputnik I*. Then he chaired the Senate committee that created NASA.

In 1960, some southern and western Democrats wanted to block John Kennedy's nomination so they supported Johnson for president. The effort failed, but in a surprising move, Kennedy chose Johnson for vice president.

Vice President Johnson was much busier than most men in his office had been in the past. He made good-will trips, sat in on cabinet meetings, and discussed legislation with Congressmen. The death of President Kennedy brought great sadness to the nation, but Johnson was unusually well prepared to take over as president, and for a time, his popularity was very high.

JOHNSON AS PRESIDENT (first term). Johnson was determined to be a president who got things accomplished. Johnson knew he had less than a year to convince the voters he was worthy of their votes, so he pressured his former colleagues in the House and Senate to pass bills quickly. Important legislation, long-buried in committee, was suddenly brought to a vote.

The Civil Rights Act of 1964 overcame strong opposition in the Senate with the help of Republican Senator Everett Dirksen. The act made it illegal to bar anyone from a hotel, restaurant, barbershop, or place of amusement on the basis of their race. It cut off federal programs to any community that allowed discrimination.

Taxes were reduced by over $11 billion. Congress voted money to combat poverty. Job training programs were increased, and more money was put into federal education programs.

The election of 1964. In 1964, the presidential candidates represented opposite views on almost every major topic. Barry Goldwater was a conservative Republican senator from Arizona. He had voted against the Civil Rights Act, wanted to make Social Security voluntary, and was critical of the TVA and many other government programs.

Johnson won the election by 27 million popular votes and by 486–52 in electoral votes. Democrats also gained more seats in Congress, with 295 to 140 in the House and 68 to 32 in the Senate. The Republicans had carried only six states, five of those in the south, marking the beginning of a strong Republican presence in the south.

JOHNSON AS PRESIDENT (second term). Johnson's second term began with the passage of Medicare, a program to help the elderly pay for medical expenses. There were new, large grants for education. A program to help Appalachia was approved. The amount being used to fight poverty was doubled. The Voting Rights Act was passed in 1965 to protect African Americans' rights to register and vote. The Twenty-fourth Amendment was ratified, making the poll tax unconstitutional.

In 1966, the record of successes began to develop a backlash. The public was beginning to wonder if bigger programs and more government involvement had gone too far. In the election of 1966, the Democrats lost 47 seats in the House and three in the Senate.

Two major problems divided Americans for many years to come.

Race. Johnson's efforts to solve the unfairness in the way African Americans were treated had centered on the south. However, many blacks living in northern cities faced different problems. Young blacks in the north began forming militant groups that spoke in terms of revolution and violence. Riots broke out in northern cities. The worst riot was in the Watts section of Los Angeles, which left 34 dead, hundreds injured, and many buildings burned.

The Kerner Commission studied the racial tension, and said in its 1968 report: "Our nation is moving toward two societies, one black, one white—separate but unequal."

Vietnam. The war in Vietnam had been going on since 1947. At first, the rebels wanted to drive the French out, and they succeeded in 1954. Vietnam was divided that year between the Communists in North Vietnam led by Ho Chi Minh and the anti-Communist government in South Vietnam, with its capital in Saigon. President Kennedy had previously sent a few thousand troops to help train the South Vietnamese army, but their efforts had failed. Now a group of anti-American Communist rebels in the south, who were called the Viet Cong, were fighting against the South Vietnamese army and the Americans. Supplies from the Communists in the north were being sent through neighboring Cambodia and Laos to help the Viet Cong.

Johnson waited until after the 1964 election to send larger numbers of troops to Vietnam, with the purpose of showing so much force that North Vietnam would make peace. In November 1965, there were 165,000 U.S. troops in Vietnam; and more were being sent. By 1968, the number had reached 543,000. Despite predictions that victory was around the corner, victory seemed no nearer than before.

Protests by college students soon to be drafted became a common occurrence. The famous boxer Muhammad Ali refused to be inducted into the army. That inspired others to burn their draft cards or flee to Canada to avoid the draft.

Johnson's popularity was dropping, both in Congress and on the streets. In 1968, he announced he would not run for another term.

In April, Dr. King was assassinated in Memphis, Tennessee, and after winning the California presidential primary that summer, Robert Kennedy was assassinated. Johnson's vice president, Hubert Humphrey, was defeated in 1968, and the former vice president, Richard Nixon, was elected.

Name: _____ Date: _____

Recalling Key Details

Directions: Answer the following questions using what you have learned from the reading selection.

True/False:

Write *T* if the statement is true or *F* if it is false.

_____ 1. Lyndon Johnson served in the navy while he was in the U.S. House of Representatives.

_____ 2. Johnson supported Truman's handling of the Korean War.

_____ 3. Johnson had very little to do as Kennedy's vice president.

_____ 4. Johnson was able to get the Civil Rights Act of 1964 passed, which outlawed discrimination on the basis of race in many public places.

_____ 5. Johnson decreased the number of U.S. troops in Vietnam.

Multiple Choice:

6. Which of these was not passed during Johnson's administration?
   A. Americans With Disabilities Act
   B. Voting Rights Act
   C. Medicare
   D. Civil Rights Act

7. Which group did the United States support in the Vietnam War?
   A. North Vietnamese army
   B. Viet Cong
   C. South Vietnamese army
   D. Cambodian army

8. African Americans in the north formed groups that pushed what?
   A. Peaceful demonstrations
   B. Sit-ins
   C. Voting reform
   D. Revolution

Structured Response:

9. After all the success in getting legislation passed to help the civil rights movement, the poor, and the elderly, why did public opinion turn against Johnson?

   _____

   _____

   _____

10. What was the reasoning behind sending such large numbers of troops to Vietnam?

   _____

   _____

   _____

RICHARD NIXON
(1913–1994, P. 1969–1974)

Richard Nixon was born in Yorba Linda, California, in 1913, into a poor but hardworking family. Richard graduated from Whittier College as student body president in 1934, and he received a scholarship to Duke University School of Law, from which he graduated in 1937. He married Thelma Catherine (Pat) Ryan in 1940. After five years of practicing law, he joined the navy in 1942 and was sent to the Pacific as an officer. He was discharged in 1946.

He ran for Congress in 1946 as a Republican and was named to the House Un-American Activities Committee (HUAC). There, he became famous for his attacks on Alger Hiss, a former State Department official accused of having been a Communist. In 1950, Nixon was elected to the U.S. Senate. In 1952, conservative Republicans saw him as a good running mate for Dwight Eisenhower, a middle-of-the-road Republican.

Nixon was accused of having $18,000 of his living expenses as a senator paid for by a group of wealthy businessmen. He appeared on television with his wife Pat, his two daughters, and his dog Checkers to deny the claim. He stated that the only gift he had received was the dog, which had been given to his daughters. The public supported keeping Nixon on the ticket.

As vice president, he was sent as Eisenhower's representative into some tough situations. On one trip to Latin America, his motorcade was surrounded by angry protesters who rocked his limousine back and forth.

In 1960, Nixon ran for president against John Kennedy and lost by a small margin. Two years later, he lost his run for governor of California. At that point, he was ready to quit politics, and he told the press, whom he blamed for his defeat, "Now you won't have Nixon to kick around anymore." However, by 1964, he was campaigning hard for Goldwater, and Nixon was rewarded with the party nomination for president in 1968.

The campaign of 1968. Nixon chose Maryland's governor, Spiro Agnew, as his vice president. Nixon's Democratic opponent was Vice President Hubert Humphrey, who had difficulty getting support from those who supported the Vietnam War while still trying to win over those who were against it. A third candidate, George Wallace, created a new ticket, the American Independence Party, which was against integration of schools and in favor of law and order. In electoral votes, Nixon won by 301–191 over Humphrey; Wallace came in third with a respectable 46 electoral votes. In the popular vote, Nixon won by only a half-million votes over Humphrey.

NIXON AS PRESIDENT (first term). Nixon had been elected president, but the Democrats controlled Congress. Although he could not always control spending, Nixon simply refused to spend all the money that had been budgeted for some programs. He rarely called cabinet meetings and ignored many of his "official" cabinet. Instead, he turned to other advisors, some of whom became especially important. Henry Kissinger, a Harvard professor, became his National Security Advisor; H.R. Haldeman, an advertising executive, became his chief of staff; John Mitchell, another close friend, was named attorney general.

Inflation became a serious issue during Nixon's first term because of the cost of fighting the Vietnam War, rising food prices, and the cost of gasoline. OPEC, a group of oil producing countries, began cutting back on production, and oil prices increased slowly at first, then jumped quickly in 1973.

Nixon wanted conservatives on the Supreme Court who would be likely to support his positions on limiting defendants' rights and other issues. Warren Burger, a moderate, was chosen as chief justice. Then the Senate rejected two men he chose for associate justice vacancies. Nixon then chose three other able men to fill vacancies. However, Supreme Court justices sometimes make decisions that surprise, and even oppose, the president who chose them.

Foreign policy. Nixon had always been strongly anti-Communist, but as president, he and his foreign affairs advisor, Dr. Henry Kissinger, began to change United States policies that had been held since the beginning of the Cold War.

Nixon began pulling U.S. troops out of South Vietnam and relying on bombing attacks on the North to end the war. U.S. troop numbers dropped from 543,000 to 39,000 in 1972.

The Soviet Union and China were clearly unfriendly with each other, and Nixon saw an opportunity to improve relations with China. In 1972, he made a trip to China that went well. A few months later, he visited Moscow, and agreements were made to limit arms and increase trade.

The election of 1972. Nixon was going strong by 1972, and Republicans were united behind him. The Democrats, on the other hand, were divided into warring camps. Older Democrats preferred Ted Kennedy, Edmund Muskie, or Hubert Humphrey. Young Democrats rallied behind Senator George McGovern, who was anti-Vietnam War. McGovern was chosen as the party candidate, however, nothing went right for McGovern. Because other speakers droned on, he could not give his acceptance speech until 3:00 A.M. His running mate, Senator Thomas Eagleton, was dropped because he had once had electric shock treatments for depression. After burglars were caught inside Democratic headquarters at the Watergate complex, McGovern charged that it was a Republican plot, but most Americans assumed he was just grasping at straws. The McGovern campaign was starved for money, while big donations flooded into Nixon headquarters. The election was a clear victory for Nixon, who received over 60 percent of the popular vote; McGovern won only in Massachusetts and the District of Columbia.

NIXON AS PRESIDENT (second term). The glory of the moment was short, however. In 1973, Vice President Agnew was forced to resign because of criminal charges brought against him. Nixon chose Gerald Ford as his new vice president.

Vietnam. To help South Vietnam, which was losing badly to the North, Nixon began bombing attacks on Viet Cong supply lines through Laos and Cambodia. Anti-war campus demonstrations began again, and at Kent State University in Ohio, National Guardsmen killed four students.

Watergate. For the 1972 campaign, Nixon had assembled a group of zealous supporters willing to do anything to win. Heading the Committee to Re-Elect the President (dubbed CREEP) was former Attorney General Mitchell. A group was sent to Democratic headquarters to plant listening devices. They were caught and sentenced to 20 years in prison. One of those convicted told the judge they had been sent by CREEP. Others began to talk to save themselves. Another said conversations had been held in the president's office to cover up CREEP's part in the affair. Mitchell and Nixon denied this, but then it was learned there was a taping machine in the office.

The Supreme Court in a 9–0 decision ordered Nixon to turn over some of the tapes to a special prosecutor. When the contents were revealed, impeachment proceedings were begun by the House. The House Judiciary Committee voted to impeach the president, and Nixon resigned rather than face an impeachment vote by the full House and a Senate trial. Trials for Watergate defendants continued for months, and many of those involved served prison time. Nixon was pardoned by President Ford.

Nixon lived long enough after leaving office to improve his reputation, and he gave helpful advice to other presidents on foreign affairs. He died on April 22, 1994.

Name: _____ Date: _____

Recalling Key Details

Directions: Answer the following questions using what you have learned from the reading selection.

Matching:

___ 1. Committee that tried to find Communists in government

___ 2. Committee formed to get Richard Nixon reelected

___ 3. Group that raised oil prices in the early 1970s

___ 4. House committee that voted to impeach Nixon

___ 5. Dog given to Nixon's daughters

A. Checkers

B. Judiciary

C. OPEC

D. CREEP

E. HUAC

Multiple Choice:

6. Who rejected Nixon's conservative choices to the Supreme Court?

   A. The Chief Justice

   C. The House

   B. The Senate

   D. The Cabinet

7. Where did Nixon travel to improve relations with communist nations?

   A. Vietnam

   C. The Soviet Union

   B. Cuba

   D. China

8. What was supposed to be planted at the Democratic headquarters in the Watergate complex?

   A. Listening devices

   C. Incriminating evidence

   B. A bomb

   D. Scandalous photographs

Structured Response:

9. How did Nixon handle the Vietnam War?

_____

_____

_____

_____

_____

10. What evidence was there that Nixon had talked about CREEP's role in the Watergate affair?

_____

_____

_____

_____

_____

GERALD FORD
(1913–2006, P. 1974–1977)

Born Leslie King in Omaha, Nebraska, Gerald R. Ford was adopted and renamed by his stepfather. He grew up in Grand Rapids, Michigan. He was a star football player and received a football scholarship to the University of Michigan where he was the most valuable player in 1934. Yale University hired him as an assistant coach, making it possible for him to attend Yale Law School. He graduated in the top third of his class in 1941 and returned to Grand Rapids to practice law.

In 1942, Ford joined the navy and was an officer in the South Pacific. After World War II, he returned to Grand Rapids and married Elizabeth (Betty) Bloomer. She and Gerald had three sons and one daughter. He was elected to the U.S. House of Representatives in 1948 and served for 13 terms. A conservative Republican, he served as minority leader in the House for eight years.

In 1973, Vice President Agnew was forced to resign, and President Nixon chose Ford as the new vice president. He was approved by both Houses of Congress. Soon President Nixon was fighting charges of covering up the Watergate break-in and resigned to avoid impeachment. On August 9, 1974, Ford took the presidential oath of office, having never been elected to be vice president or president. Ford chose Nelson Rockefeller, former governor of New York, for vice president.

FORD AS PRESIDENT. In a controversial move, Ford granted a pardon to President Nixon in September 1974, explaining that it was to begin the national healing process after Watergate and to save Nixon and his family from further suffering. He also granted amnesty (forgiveness) for many of those who had evaded the draft or deserted from the armed forces during the Vietnam War.

Domestic policies. Ford faced an economy with high unemployment and inflation. He tried to control inflation by cutting some government programs and vetoed attempts to restore money to the budget. During his time in office, inflation dropped from 11.2 percent to 5.3 percent. In 1975, he proposed tax cuts, but Congress failed to approve most of his efforts.

Foreign affairs. With Henry Kissinger as his secretary of state, Ford worked to improve relations with the Soviet Union. In 1975, he traveled to Helsinki, Finland, where he signed an agreement with the Soviets promising to honor European borders.

Despite the United States pumping more aid into South Vietnam and Cambodia, by April 1975, the governments of both countries had fallen. In mid-April, Cambodia surrendered to Communist forces. Airlifts of Vietnamese children and adults out of South Vietnam began. By April 27, Saigon was being shelled, and Ford ordered a helicopter evacuation of those Americans still in Vietnam. The last helicopters left April 29 as Communist forces entered the capital city. South Vietnam surrendered the next day. The war had cost the United States nearly 58,000 men and $150 billion.

The election of 1976. During two separate incidents while campaigning in California, women tried to shoot the president, but he was not injured. Ford narrowly won the Republican nomination for president. The Democratic candidate, former Governor Jimmy Carter of Georgia, appealed to many as an outsider who was not part of the Washington crowd. Ford lost the popular vote by 1.7 million and the electoral vote by 240 to 297.

After the Fords left public life, Mrs. Ford was treated for alcoholism. She later started the Betty Ford Center in 1982, which has treated many people for addictions. The Fords retired to southern California. Ford died on December 25, 2006, at the age of 93.

Name: _____ Date: _____

Recalling Key Details

Directions: Answer the following questions using what you have learned from the reading selection.

Matching:

____ 1. School where Gerald Ford served as an assistant coach and earned his law degree.

____ 2. School where Ford was the most valuable football player

____ 3. Where Ford served in the navy during World War II

____ 4. Where Ford signed an agreement with Soviet leaders

____ 5. Capital of South Vietnam that fell to the Communists in 1975

A. South Pacific

B. Helsinki

C. University of Michigan

D. Saigon

E. Yale University

Multiple Choice:

6. What leadership position did Ford hold in the House of Representatives?
   A. Speaker of the house
   B. Majority leader
   C. Minority leader
   D. President pro tempore

7. Which two people did Ford replace in their offices?
   A. Secretary of State Henry Kissinger
   B. President Richard Nixon
   C. Attorney General John Mitchell
   D. Vice President Spiro Agnew

8. Who were granted amnesty by President Ford?
   A. Draft evaders
   B. Escaped convicts
   C. Petty criminals
   D. Attempted assassins

Structured Response:

9. What did Ford give as his reasons for pardoning former President Nixon?

   _____

   _____

   _____

   _____

10. What happened in Cambodia and South Vietnam in 1975?

    _____

    _____

    _____

    _____

JIMMY CARTER
(1924–   , P. 1977–1981)

Jimmy Carter was born in Plains, Georgia, in 1924. He was the son of a well-to-do farmer whose African-American farm workers lived in small cottages nearby. His father strongly favored segregation, but his mother was kind and open with the workers. Jimmy took after his mother on this and became a good friend to many African Americans.

Jimmy set an early goal of graduating from the Naval Academy at Annapolis. In 1941, he entered Georgia Southwestern College while waiting for a letter inviting him to attend the Naval Academy. The letter finally arrived, but he would not be able to enter the Academy until the summer of 1943. He switched to Georgia Tech and was accepted into the NROTC unit there to prepare for Annapolis. The Naval Academy was tough for the students, but Carter studied hard. On leave before his third year at the Academy, he fell in love with Rosalynn Smith. Graduating in the top 10 percent of his class, Carter received his commission as an ensign and married Rosalynn in 1946.

After serving on surface ships for two years, Carter chose to enter the submarine service. He became an expert on subs, and was proud of his record. He then worked under Admiral Hyman Rickover, a legend in the navy for his work on building the submarine service. From Rickover, Carter learned the importance of detailed planning.

When his father died in 1953 and his mother asked him to take over the family farm, Carter resigned from the navy and returned to Plains in 1954. He built up the family's peanut-growing operation. The Carters had three sons and a daughter, Amy, who grew up in the White House during her father's administration.

Carter was elected to the Georgia Senate in 1962, failed to win the governor's race in 1966, but won in 1970. He improved efficiency in government and started new social programs without increasing taxes. In 1972, Carter began exploring the possibility of running for president while speaking around the United States as chairman of the Democratic Campaign Committee.

The campaign of 1976. Carter was a unique candidate for president. He started out with little money, and no one had heard of him in the early primary states. He was not apologetic about being a "born-again" Christian, strongly motivated by religion. His campaign was about character, and he wanted government to represent the honest and decent side of Americans. He was the outsider untarnished by scandals.

President Ford fought off a challenge from Ronald Reagan for the Republican nomination, but Carter won a narrow victory over Ford in the election. He won the popular vote by only about 2% and the electoral vote 297 to 240.

CARTER AS PRESIDENT. Instead of riding home from his inauguration, Carter and his family walked, waving to people along the way. He preferred the informal approach. Instead of focusing on one problem, he often proposed many programs at one time. Since he had not been a member of Congress, he had few relationships to call on and did not feel the need to play the political game. Unfortunately, Congress felt the same way about cooperating with him. Even though he was dealing with a Democratic House and Senate, Congress was slow to respond to his requests.

Domestic affairs. Carter had criticized Ford for high inflation and unemployment. Despite Carter's efforts, prices kept going up, reaching 20 percent inflation in 1980. It now took $1 to buy what would have cost 15 cents in 1940.

Part of the reason for higher prices was the cost of energy, especially oil and electricity. Nuclear power plants had been seen as the way to cut energy costs, but a nuclear accident at Three Mile Island in Pennsylvania caused a near-tragedy. Congress finally approved a program to cut dependence on foreign oil by promoting programs to produce more coal, solar, and wind-produced electricity. Congress passed the Energy Security Act in 1980, and a "superfund" was established for cleaning up dangerous chemicals spilled or dumped in the environment.

Carter was able to reorganize the executive branch to make government more efficient. Two new cabinet-level departments were added during Carter's administration: the Department of Energy and the Department of Education. He signed civil service reform into law in 1978.

Foreign affairs. Carter was concerned about human rights and was very critical of nations that abused their own citizens. He listed South Africa, North Korea, and the Soviet Union, among others, as the worst offenders.

The Panama Canal had been a trouble spot for President Ford, and he had been strongly criticized by conservative Republicans when he suggested it should be given to Panama to control. The issue was still being argued when Carter became president. It was only with great effort that a treaty was made to turn the Canal over to Panama by the year 2000.

U.S. relations with China improved, and the two nations began exchanging ambassadors; trade between the United States and China began. However, U.S. relations with the Soviet Union worsened after Soviet troops moved into Afghanistan in December 1979. Carter announced a trade embargo on many Soviet goods, and the United States led an international boycott of the 1980 Olympic Games in Moscow, which was unpopular with the American people. A new strategic arms limitations treaty (SALT II) was signed by Carter and Soviet President Leonid Brezhnev in 1979, but after the invasion of Afghanistan, the treaty was withdrawn from the Senate, and it was never ratified.

Carter's greatest success was in bringing Israeli Prime Minister Menachem Begin and Egyptian President Anwar al-Sadat to talks at Camp David, which resulted in the peace treaty signed in 1979.

Carter's greatest defeat was in relations with Iran. Anti-American Muslim leaders, led by the Ayatollah Khomeini, had overthrown the Shah (ruler) of Iran. With government approval, Iranian students stormed the U.S. embassy in Tehran, captured the 52 Americans there, and held them hostage. U.S. efforts to rescue the hostages failed. The Iranian hostage crisis became a symbol of Carter's failures. The hostages were not released until after Ronald Reagan's inauguration on January 20, 1981, after 444 days. Carter was able to greet the freed hostages in West Germany as a special envoy of President Reagan.

Jimmy Carter has remained one of the most active ex-presidents in history. His peace-keeping and humanitarian efforts since leaving office have led to a favorable opinion of Carter worldwide. In 1982, Jimmy and Rosalynn established the Carter Center in Atlanta, Georgia, to advance human rights and alleviate unnecessary human suffering. He and Rosalynn have been active in the Habitat for Humanity organization, building homes for low-income people. In 1994, Carter was sent on peace-keeping missions to Haiti and North Korea by President Bill Clinton. He was awarded the Presidential Medal of Freedom in 1999. Carter met with Fidel Castro of Cuba in 2002. He has also worked to promote fair elections in South America, Europe, Africa, and the Middle East. In 2002, Carter received the Nobel Peace Prize for his work through the Carter Center "to find peaceful solutions to international conflicts, to advance democracy and human rights, and to promote economic and social development."

Name: _____ Date: _____

Recalling Key Details

Directions: Answer the following questions using what you have learned from the reading selection.

Matching:

____ 1. Type of vessel Jimmy Carter served on in the navy
____ 2. Product Carter was known for raising on his farm
____ 3. The biggest economic problem during Carter's administration
____ 4. Money for cleaning up environmental chemical spills
____ 5. A restriction on buying goods from the Soviet Union

A. inflation
B. embargo
C. peanuts
D. submarine
E. superfund

Multiple Choice:

6. Which new executive departments were added during Carter's administration?
   A. Department of Education
   B. Department of Defense
   C. Department of Homeland Security
   D. Department of Energy

7. A treaty to turn over what transportation asset to its home country was signed by Carter?
   A. Suez Canal
   B. Panama Canal
   C. Berlin Wall
   D. St. Lawrence Seaway

8. American hostages were held for 444 days in what country during the Carter presidency?
   A. The Soviet Union
   B. Egypt
   C. Afghanistan
   D. Iran

Structured Response:

9. What was Carter's greatest success in foreign relations?

_____

_____

_____

_____

10. Even though Carter had several failures during his presidency, why does he have an excellent reputation around the world today?

_____

_____

_____

_____

_____

RONALD REAGAN
(1911–2004, P. 1981–1989)

Ronald Reagan grew up in Dixon, Illinois. His father was an alcoholic and held poor-paying jobs. Ronald sold popcorn at high school games and worked as a lifeguard in the summer to earn the money to attend college. Reagan played football and was in college theatrical productions while attending Eureka College in Illinois; he received his degree in 1932. After graduating, he became a well-known radio sportscaster in Des Moines, Iowa.

In 1937, Warner Brothers hired Reagan as an actor. During World War II, he enlisted in the army and made training and morale-boosting films. He held the rank of captain when he was discharged. After the war, Reagan returned to Hollywood, but his movie career was not successful. Fortunately, television was growing, and he became a host introducing popular television shows.

Reagan had two children with actress Jane Wyman, one of whom died shortly after birth, and they also adopted a son. The marriage ended in divorce. He then married actress Nancy Davis in 1952, and the couple also had two children.

Although he had been a Roosevelt New Deal Democrat, Reagan began to change into a conservative Republican. He had become fed up watching lazy civil service employees during the war. He was also concerned about Communist influence in the film industry while he served as president of the Screen Actors Guild.

Wealthy Republicans suggested that Reagan run for governor of California in 1966. He promised to cut taxes and won by over a million votes. He was unable to persuade the legislature to lower taxes, but he learned to work with the legislature and to use television as a method of gaining public support. He tried unsuccessfully in 1972 and 1976 to win the Republican nomination for president.

The election of 1980. The Democrats were split between those who liked Carter and the liberals who liked Ted Kennedy. Reagan also had competition: John Anderson and George H. W. Bush. Reagan prevailed, and then he chose Bush for vice president. Anderson went on to form a new National Unity Party.

The themes of the campaign were clear. Carter believed the nation was in a mess and needed his leadership. Reagan believed the problem was Carter. In their debate, Reagan asked the public: "Are you better off than you were four years ago?" The Reagan victory was even greater than anyone anticipated. He not only had 489 electoral votes to Carter's 49, but he also won by 8.3 million popular votes. Anderson received only seven percent of the popular vote.

REAGAN AS PRESIDENT. Reagan was cheerful and optimistic. He was known as the "Great Communicator." Even when he was rolled into the operating room for a gunshot wound after an assassination attempt on March 30, 1981, he asked if the surgeons were all good Republicans.

Reagan's approach was to speak in general outlines while his officials worked out the details. When problems occurred, the official was the one in trouble with the public and press, not the president. His critics began calling him the "Teflon president" because he rarely got the blame for mistakes.

Economic problems. Reagan's solution for high Inflation and unemployment was called "supply side economics." He would reduce taxes to encourage business expansion. In 1981, taxes dropped five percent, and in 1982 and 1983, another ten percent. The government cut costs by reducing social programs like welfare benefits, unemployment compensation, low-cost housing, and grants for college students. At the same time, he was determined to increase defense spending, which by 1985 had reached $300 billion. Tax money never came close to paying the cost of government, and the budget deficit rose from $74 billion in 1980 to $221 billion in 1986. In 1982, the worst recession in many years occurred, and thousands of workers were unemployed, but by the next year, conditions had improved.

The election of 1984. The Democratic candidate, former Vice President Walter Mondale, chose as his running mate the first woman to run on a national ticket, Geraldine Ferraro. Mondale was never able to gain much momentum in the campaign, and he lost to Reagan by 525–13 in electoral votes and by nearly 17 million popular votes.

Foreign policy. In 1985, the Reagan Doctrine said we would help any nation that was struggling against Communism. The United States became involved in many trouble spots around the world.

In Afghanistan, a civil war was going on between the Communist-controlled government supported by the Soviet Union and Afghan Muslim rebels. The United States sent support to the Afghan rebels.

Libya was ruled by Muammar Gaddafi, who was suspected of using his oil money to help terrorist groups in other countries. The United States found that he was helping terrorists in Germany, and American planes dropped bombs on some Libyan cities.

Iran and Iraq were at war, and the United States helped Iraq by guarding the Persian Gulf. One of the U.S. ships was attacked by an Iraqi plane. In 1988, the United States shot down an Iranian airliner by accident.

Central America. The United States supported an unpopular government in El Salvador that was fighting rebels. Congress sent help to a new leader elected in 1983. In October 1983, Reagan sent U.S. troops to the island nation of Grenada when a coup overthrew the Communist leader. The troops quickly got the situation under control and democratic elections were held in 1984. Rebels called Contras were also trying to overthrow the Communist Sandinistas that controlled Nicaragua. Congress passed laws against sending military aid to the Contras. To get around the law, a group of White House officials arranged for supplies to be sold to Iran at a very low price, then in turn, Iran sent aid to the Contras. The Iran-Contra Scandal was eventually discovered, but no one was sure whether Reagan had known what was happening.

When dealing with the Soviet Union, at first it looked as if Reagan was preparing for a war with the "evil empire," as he called it. Pershing II missiles were set up in West Germany that could reach Soviet targets in five minutes. The Soviets began building up their military power as well. Reagan pushed a new weapons system called the Strategic Defense Initiative (SDI). This program would put satellites in space, capable of shooting down incoming missiles. Critics called it a "Star Wars" defense that would never work. In time, Reagan's attitude toward the Soviets softened. The influence of Secretary of State George Schultz and changes in the Kremlin may have led to the shift in attitude. When Mikhail Gorbachev was chosen as Soviet premier, he began changes that eventually led to democracy. He was eager to develop better relations with the United States. Reagan saw the changes as good for peace, and he attended meetings in Switzerland and Iceland with the Soviet leader. Agreements were made to destroy many of the missiles on both sides. While neither side was prepared to call off the Cold War completely, great progress was made.

Reagan returned to private life as a very popular person. After several years of retirement, Reagan developed Alzheimer's disease and remained out of the public eye. He died on June 5, 2004, at his Bel Air, California, home.

Name: _____ Date: _____

Recalling Key Details

Directions: Answer the following questions using what you have learned from the reading selection.

Matching:

_____ 1. Ronald Reagan's nickname that indicated he was charming and could use his TV personality to gain public support

_____ 2. Reagan's term for the Soviet Union

_____ 3. Reagan nickname for his ability to escape blame for mistakes

_____ 4. What critics called the Strategic Defense Initiative

_____ 5. Reagan's solution to high inflation and unemployment

A. the "evil empire"

B. the "Teflon president"

C. the "Great Communicator"

D. "supply-side economics"

E. "Star Wars" defense

Multiple Choice:

6. Which programs were cut in order to reduce government costs?
   A. Welfare benefits
   B. Defense spending
   C. Unemployment compensation
   D. Grants for college students

7. The Reagan Doctrine said the United States would help any nation struggling against what?
   A. Inflation
   B. Communism
   C. Unemployment
   D. Rebels

8. The Iran-Contra Scandal involved selling supplies to Iran and then having Iran send aid to rebels in what country?
   A. El Salvador
   B. Iraq
   C. Granada
   D. Nicaragua

Structured Response:

9. Why did it look like the United States and the Soviet Union might go to war?

   _____

   _____

   _____

   _____

10. How did things change in relations between the United States and the Soviet Union?

   _____

   _____

   _____

GEORGE H. W. BUSH
(1924–2018, P. 1989–1993)

George Herbert Walker Bush was born into the very wealthy family of Prescott Bush in 1924. As a boy, George attended Phillips Academy. Anxious to volunteer during World War II, he lied about his age to get into the naval aviation program, and he became a pilot at 18. From 1942 to 1945, he flew 58 missions in the Pacific. During one mission he was shot down. For heroism, he was awarded the Distinguished Flying Cross. In 1945, he married Barbara Pierce, the daughter of a magazine publisher. The Bushes had six children. Their daughter Robin died of leukemia at age 3.

After the war, he attended Yale University where he captained the baseball team. Bush graduated with high grades. Instead of going into his father's investment business, the Bushes moved to Texas where he started his own oil company. Bush lost a race for the Senate in 1964, but he won a House seat in 1966 and 1968. In 1970, he lost in his second try for a Senate seat. President Nixon appointed him United Nations ambassador from 1971 to 1972. In 1973–1974, he was chairman of the Republican National Committee. In 1974–1975, he was chief liaison officer in Peking, and he was director of the CIA in 1976–1977. After trying unsuccessfully to win the Republican presidential nomination in 1980, he became Ronald Reagan's vice president.

The election of 1988. In 1988, Reagan's popularity was very high, and that helped Bush win the nomination. For vice president, he chose a conservative, Senator Dan Quayle, from Indiana. The Democrats chose Governor Michael Dukakis of Massachusetts as their candidate. During the campaign, Bush assured the voters: "Read my lips—no new taxes." The Dukakis campaign stumbled from the beginning, and Bush easily defeated him 426–112 in electoral votes.

BUSH AS PRESIDENT. Bush began his term with a slow start since Democrats controlled both Houses of Congress. Among his cabinet members were James Baker, secretary of state; Dick Cheney, secretary of defense; and Elizabeth Dole, secretary of labor.

In 1989, with revenues dropping because of a slowing economy and high deficits, Bush reluctantly agreed to a tax hike, breaking his "Read my lips" promise. A recession in 1991 resulted from a drop in profits and less buying by consumers. Businesses began laying off workers, and unemployment jumped from 5.5 percent in 1990 to 6.5 percent in 1991 to 7.4 percent in 1992. The federal government also had to rescue some savings and loans that had made unwise loans.

Foreign affairs. In 1988, a U.S. grand jury indicted General Noriega of Panama for drug trafficking. After 24,000 U.S. troops were involved in an attempt to capture Noriega, he surrendered himself in January 1990 and was convicted in Miami of drug trafficking.

The breakup of the Soviet Union. Since the Truman era, the Soviet Union and United States had engaged in the Cold War. By the time Bush came into office, the Soviets were falling behind in the arms race, and their economy was in a state of confusion. As conditions in the Soviet Union worsened every day, the Communist Party lost control over the Soviet block countries around it and the leadership of those countries. On November 9, 1989, Germans were able to tear down portions of the wall dividing East and West Berlin without interference from the military. The reunification of East and West Germany began soon after. Boris Yeltsin, leader of Russia's Soviet Socialist Republic, left the Communist Party and was elected president of the Russian Soviet Socialist Republic. On

December 25, 1991, Mikhail Gorbachev resigned as President of the Soviet Union, and the Union of Soviet Socialist Republics dissolved. The republics that had made up the U.S.S.R. were given the choice of leaving and forming independent nations or remaining in a new Commonwealth of Independent States. Estonia, Latvia, and Lithuania left, and President Bush recognized them in December 1991.

The Persian Gulf War. From 1980 to 1988, Iraq and its neighbor, Iran, fought a war that killed thousands on both sides. After the war, the ruler of Iraq, Saddam Hussein, found his nation in deep financial trouble. He wanted an easy victory to restore his reputation as a great leader in the Muslim world. In 1990, he threatened, then seized, the small, oil-rich neighbor country Kuwait. To frighten Saudi Arabia, he moved troops to the Arabian border. Other countries in the region gave their support to the Saudis, and the United States quickly sent a fleet, troops, and arms to support the Saudis. Israel was also in danger of attack by Iraqi Scud missiles, so the United States sent Patriot missiles to Israel and Saudi Arabia to shoot down the Scuds. The United Nations condemned Iraq, and many nations sent troops to form a 600,000-man coalition army and air force surrounding Iraq.

Hussein rejected all demands that he pull out of Kuwait. On January 10, 1991, Congress authorized the use of force against Iraq. Operation "Desert Storm," or what became known as the first Persian Gulf War, began a week later with air attacks. Iraq's capital, Baghdad, was hit with missiles and bombs that destroyed most of its communications operations. Iraq's Scud missiles were fired at Israel and Saudi Arabia, but most were destroyed by Patriot missiles.

In his State of the Union Address, Bush warned that Iraq would be invaded unless it pulled out of Kuwait. Land fighting began on February 24, with 200,000 troops taking part in the attack. Coalition troops moved into Kuwait and Iraq. Retreating Iraqi forces set fire to many oil facilities before leaving Kuwait. They then began dumping oil into the Persian Gulf, creating an oil slick 60 miles long and 20 miles wide. On February 27, Bush announced that Kuwait was freed and Iraq's army defeated. The land war had lasted 100 hours, but Iraqi losses had been devastating: up to 100,000 killed and wounded, 175,000 captured, and about 3,700 tanks destroyed. The United States had 148 fatalities.

Hussein was still in power, however, and he defied the rules set down by the United Nations for inspection of his atomic and bacteriological warfare plants. Many Americans were convinced that the war should have continued until Hussein was forced out of office.

The election of 1992. After the war, Bush boasted an 89 percent approval rating, but with rising unemployment and many worried about the economy, his popularity began to decline fast.

The Democrats chose Governor William (Bill) Clinton of Arkansas as their candidate. Bush easily won the Republican nomination. A third challenger, Texas billionaire Ross Perot, founded the Reform Party in an effort to reform American politics. Clinton won by 5.8 million popular votes and 370–168 electoral votes over Bush. For the first time in 12 years, a Democrat was to occupy the White House.

The Bushes retired to a new home in Houston, Texas, and often visited their vacation home in Kennebunkport, Maine. As former presidents, Bush and Bill Clinton developed a friendship when they worked together to raise funds for relief after the Asian tsunami in 2004, Hurricane Katrina in 2005, and the Haiti earthquake in 2010. Later, Bush took pride in two sons becoming governors, George W. Bush in Texas and Jeb Bush in Florida. George W. Bush would then go on to be our 43rd president. In 2011, President Barack Obama awarded Bush the Presidential Medal of Freedom. In April 2018, Barbara Bush died, and George H. W. Bush died on November 30, 2018.

Name: _____ Date: _____

Recalling Key Details

Directions: Answer the following questions using what you have learned from the reading selection.

Matching:

____ 1. George H. W. Bush's job in World War II

____ 2. Bush's role at the United Nations from 1971 to 1972

____ 3. Bush's position with the Republican National Committee

____ 4. Bush's title at the CIA in 1976–1977

____ 5. Bush's role in the Reagan administration

A. ambassador

B. director

C. pilot

D. vice president

E. chairman

Multiple Choice:

6. What happened in 1991 that resulted in high unemployment?

   A. A raise in taxes

   B. A recession

   C. The invasion of Panama

   D. The invasion of Iraq

7. What country was able to reunify after the fall of the Soviet Union?

   A. Poland

   B. Ukraine

   C. Germany

   D. Estonia

8. The United States and the other coalition countries went to war with Iraq because Saddam Hussein's forces had invaded what country on the Persian Gulf?

   A. Iran

   B. Saudi Arabia

   C. Afghanistan

   D. Kuwait

Structured Response:

9. What happened in the Soviet Union in 1991 that changed the face of world politics?

_____

_____

_____

_____

10. Why did Bush lose the 1992 election despite winning the Persian Gulf War and having such a high approval rating in 1991?

_____

_____

_____

_____

WILLIAM (BILL) CLINTON
(1946–   , P. 1993–2001)

William Jefferson Blythe III was born in Hope, Arkansas, in 1946. His father had been killed in a traffic accident three months before he was born. His mother remarried when he was four years old to Roger Clinton, and Bill later adopted his stepfather's last name. Two events of his high school years were important to him. He played saxophone in the band (which he frequently played to entertain crowds during his political career), and he visited the White House as a Boys State delegate where he got to shake hands with President John Kennedy, which resulted in his resolution to go into politics.

Clinton received his bachelor's degree in foreign service from Georgetown University in 1968. He then attended Oxford University as a Rhodes Scholar for two years. Returning to the United States, he attended Yale University where he met Hillary Rodham, a fellow student, and received his law degree from Yale in 1973. He taught law at the University of Arkansas while preparing to enter politics.

In 1974, Clinton lost his race for Congress. The next year, he married Hillary Rodham. In 1976, he was elected as the Arkansas attorney general, and he became governor in 1978. The Clinton's daughter Chelsea was born in 1980. He lost his reelection bid for governor in 1982, but then regained the office in 1986 and was governor from then until 1992.

The election of 1992. George H. W. Bush was again the presidential nominee of the Republicans. He believed government was too big and spent too much. As the Democratic nominee, Clinton focused on the economy, which was not doing well. He argued that government should play a major part in putting America to work again. The third-party candidate was Ross Perot, a billionaire who attracted much attention with his criticisms of governmental inefficiency.

Personal attacks on Clinton's character were sometimes bitter. He had avoided the draft and opposed the Vietnam War, and there were charges of infidelity and profiting from a failed Whitewater land scheme in Arkansas. However, Clinton won the election by 370–168 in electoral votes and by 5.8 million popular votes. Perot came in third with 19.7 million popular votes.

CLINTON AS PRESIDENT (first term). Clinton struggled in his first months in office. His first problem came in an argument with military leaders over allowing homosexuals to serve in the armed forces. They reached a compromise of: "Don't ask, don't tell." His budget was in trouble because of conservative demands that spending be cut and taxes lowered. Heated debates occurred over such issues as health care and welfare reform. Many of his proposals failed or were compromised, but he got the North American Free Trade Agreement (NAFTA) passed, which made trade with Mexico and Canada easier. Congress eventually approved a budget deficit bill to slow the growth of the national debt; a bill to establish a waiting period before a person could buy handguns (the Brady Bill); and AmeriCorps, a national service program.

The Republicans, led by Speaker of the House Newt Gingrich, gained control of the House and Senate in 1994. An independent counsel, Kenneth Starr, was appointed to investigate possible Clinton involvement in the Whitewater land deal. This led to investigating the firing of workers at the White House travel office, the death of a White House lawyer, and cover-ups of Clinton infidelities.

In foreign affairs, the leaders of Israel and Jordan signed a peace agreement in 1994 at the White House. In 1995, the United States joined other countries in sending peace-keeping troops to Bosnia to end the "ethnic cleansing" of the Muslim minority there by the Serbians. The president supported Boris Yeltsin against Communist critics in Russia but criticized the Russian invasion of Chechnya, a region trying to break away from Russian domination.

The election of 1996. The Republicans chose Senator Bob Dole as their candidate to oppose Clinton in 1996. Ross Perot again entered the contest but with much less support than in 1992. Most voters approved of the improved economy and didn't care much about the scandals. Clinton won over Dole by 379–159 in electoral votes and by 8.2 million popular votes.

CLINTON AS PRESIDENT (second term). The Starr investigation began looking into a sexual harassment lawsuit filed against Clinton by Paula Jones, claiming that Clinton had made unwanted advances toward her when he was governor of Arkansas. Clinton publicly denied it had ever happened. It then became known that White House intern Monica Lewinsky had had an affair with the president. Clinton testified in a televised appearance before the Starr grand jury looking into charges of perjury in the Paula Jones case. Starr reported his charges of a cover-up to Congress. The House judiciary committee brought four charges of impeachment against Clinton, but the full House only voted to pass two of the impeachment charges. The Senate trial began on January 7, 1999, and was presided over by Chief Justice Rehnquist. It ended with a not-guilty vote of 45–55 on one charge, and 50–50 on the other, far short of the two-thirds required by the Constitution to remove a president from office.

A strong economy made it possible to create 22 million jobs, and unemployment dropped to four percent in June of 2000. With welfare rolls cut and restraint in federal spending, the federal government and most states were bringing in more taxes than ever before. In July 2000, the Treasury Department announced that $221 billion would be paid on the national debt that year. It was expected that there would be a $211 billion surplus for 2000. However, a threat to the nation's economy came from rising oil prices. These were caused by OPEC nations reducing oil production and the increased popularity of fuel-wasting vehicles.

World Affairs. Terrorism was taking on new forms, and nations had to work together to capture criminals. The United States worked with other nations to try to prevent drugs from entering the country. In February 1993, the North Tower of the World Trade Center in New York City was attacked by extremist Muslims using a truck bomb. Six people were killed. On October 12, 2000, the U.S. Navy ship the USS *Cole* was bombed by terrorists while docked in a harbor in Yemen. Seventeen sailors were killed and 39 injured. It was later determined that the al-Qaeda terrorist organization, with backing from the government of Sudan, was responsible. Fearing that nations like Iraq and Libya would receive missiles and other arms from the nations of the old Soviet Union, the United States and Russia agreed to destroy many missiles.

The Clinton administration also worked to bring warring peoples together. In Northern Ireland, the United States helped bring peace between Catholics and Protestants. The United States was also involved in talks between North and South Korea. The most difficult area was still the Middle East, where the United States, led by Secretary of State Madeleine Albright and other negotiators, continued to work with Israel, the Palestinians, and other Muslim neighbors to work out an agreement. Many issues remained to be settled when the Clinton administration ended.

Bill and Hillary Clinton moved to Chappaqua, New York, after his term as president ended. He teamed with other former presidents, including George H. W. Bush, to raise funds after global natural disasters. In 2009, Clinton helped negotiate the release of two journalists imprisoned in North Korea. He also worked to rally support for Hillary as she successfully ran for U.S. Senate and had unsuccessful runs for president in 2008 and 2016.

Name: _____ Date: _____

Recalling Key Details

Directions: Answer the following questions using what you have learned from the reading selection.

Fact/Opinion:

Write *F* if the statement is a fact or *O* if it is an opinion.

_____ 1. Having the government spend more to create more jobs is the best way to stimulate the economy.

_____ 2. President George H. W. Bush wanted the government to spend less.

_____ 3. Having a third-party candidate like Ross Perot is bad for the election process.

_____ 4. When the government has a surplus of money, it should pay on the national debt.

_____ 5. There were not enough votes for the two-thirds majority needed to remove President Bill Clinton from office.

Multiple Choice:

6. Which country was not involved in the North American Free Trade Agreement (NAFTA)?
   A. Canada
   B. China
   C. United States
   D. Mexico

7. Kenneth Starr was originally appointed to investigate what?
   A. The Whitewater land deal
   B. Clinton infidelities
   C. The death of a White House lawyer
   D. Avoiding the draft

8. Among which warring peoples was the United States able to help bring peace?
   A. Israel and the Palestinians
   B. Iraq and Iran
   C. Russia and Chechnya
   D. Catholics and Protestants in Northern Ireland

Structured Response:

9. What were some examples of terrorism directed toward the United States?

   _____

   _____

   _____

   _____

10. How did Clinton use the economy to his advantage in 1992 and 1996?

   _____

   _____

   _____

GEORGE W. BUSH
(1946–   , P. 2001–2009)

George W. Bush was born in 1946, the oldest son of George H. W. and Barbara Bush, and he grew up in Midland and Houston, Texas. At age 15, he attended Phillips Academy prep school in Andover, Massachusetts. He received his bachelor's degree from Yale University and became a pilot in the Texas Air National Guard. He later earned an MBA degree from Harvard and entered the oil business in Midland, Texas.

In 1977, George W. married Laura Welch, a school librarian, and found the focus he needed in his life. Her enthusiasm for education and books, along with the birth of their twin daughters in 1981, contributed to his interest in education.

He lost a campaign for the U.S. House of Representatives seat in 1978. At that time, he recognized that he had a drinking problem and was able to get it under control.

Bush worked on his father's presidential campaign in 1988, and then became managing partner for the Texas Rangers baseball team. He was elected governor of Texas in 1994 in a close election. In 1998, he won a second term as governor by a landslide. In that same year, his brother Jeb was elected governor of Florida.

The election of 2000. As the Republican nominee for president in 2000, Bush chose Dick Cheney as his running mate. Bush described himself as a compassionate conservative and wanted limited government, personal responsibility, strong families, local control, and lower taxes. The Democratic candidate, Al Gore, was the son of a senator, had served in the U.S. Senate himself, and was the current vice president for President Clinton. The election was very close, with a controversy over Florida's electoral votes. The results were not final until December when the U.S. Supreme Court ruled against any further recounts in Florida by a 5–4 vote. This gave Florida's electoral votes to Bush. He became the first son of a president also to be elected president since John Quincy Adams. The Republicans won control of the House, and the Senate was evenly divided, with Vice President Cheney casting a vote in the case of a tie.

BUSH AS PRESIDENT (first term). Between 2001 and 2003, Bush was able to get Congress to pass tax cuts and increase the child tax credit. Critics charged that the cuts would benefit the rich more than the poor and would lead to budget deficits and cuts in social programs. Bush also supported free trade agreements with nations around the world. To improve education, the No Child Left Behind Act was signed into law. The program required states to set standards in reading and math skills for students, with testing to hold schools accountable. Spending cuts were made in Amtrak, Medicaid, and social programs. Military spending was increased to make up for the deep cuts during the Clinton administration.

September 11, 2001. On September 11, 2001, a horrendous attack on the United States was conducted by an extremist Islamic group. The attacks were conducted against innocent American citizens, against the financial infrastructure of America, and the American military infrastructure. It began when the terrorists hijacked four airliners. Two of the planes were crashed into the World Trade Center towers in New York City, destroying those buildings. A third plane was crashed into the Pentagon in Washington, D.C. The fourth hijacked airliner crashed into a field in Pennsylvania. Due to the heroic efforts of passengers on this last airliner, it did not make it to the intended destination, the White House. Some 3,000 people were killed by the attack. Congress quickly approved $54 billion to help the cities and states affected; millions were donated by Americans to help the victims' families.

The War on Terror. Those involved in the attack were terrorists linked to Osama bin Laden's al-Qaeda organization. Bin Laden was traced to Afghanistan where the Muslim radicals, the Taliban, ruled and protected him. The United States organized opposition to overthrow the Taliban. An international coalition of military forces invaded Afghanistan on October 7, 2001, with aerial bombings and eventually ground troops. The Taliban government was removed from power and al-Qaeda was driven into the mountains. While many of the al-Qaeda leaders were killed or captured, bin Laden remained at large.

Another Middle Eastern troublemaker was Saddam Hussein, the dictator of Iraq. Hussein had maintained control of Iraq after the first Persian Gulf War, but he was under the watchful eyes of the United States and the United Nations. President Bush charged that Hussein had sent financial help to al-Qaeda and was storing weapons of mass destruction. In March 2003, the United States, Great Britain, and a coalition of 43 other countries launched an air and ground attack on Iraq that was highly successful. However, no weapons of mass destruction were ever found. Hussein was eventually captured in December 2003. He was tried by an Iraqi special tribunal and executed December 30, 2006.

The Iraq war was unpopular in the Muslim world, and radicals joined the insurgents there in guerrilla warfare against the United States and its allies. U.S. troops remained in Afghanistan and Iraq to help set up new governments there. In both countries, free elections were held, despite terrorist threats, and interim governments were set up.

In the United States, the possibility of more terrorism led to forming the cabinet-level Department of Homeland Security. Security was tightened at airports and on aircraft, as well as at other parts of the country's infrastructure, such as power plants, railroads, and water treatment facilities.

The election of 2004. In 2004, George W. Bush was reelected with a 53 percent popular majority, defeating the Democratic Senator John Kerry and his running mate Senator John Edwards. Bush received the largest number of votes of any candidate in U.S. history.

BUSH AS PRESIDENT (second term). The Republicans dominated both houses of Congress. Bush wanted to privatize Social Security, giving workers the choice of paying into the program or investing part of their money in private funds. He proposed cuts in social programs like Medicaid, transportation, and farm subsidies. All these ideas had opposition in Congress. The U.S. national debt grew due to the added expense of fighting terrorism, the wars in Iraq and Afghanistan, and expanding some government programs. To ease the nation's dependency on foreign oil, Bush's proposal to drill for oil in Alaska passed, despite environmental concerns.

In 2007, President Bush was confronted with a new challenge. The widespread practice of banks lending people more than they could afford to pay back for housing purchases triggered a financial collapse. Many families lost their homes due to foreclosures, and several large banks failed. Emergency measures passed in 2008 provided tax refunds for lower- and middle-class families, provided more funding for government-backed mortgage lenders to try to help homeowners threatened by foreclosure, and authorized spending up to $700 billion to prop up the remaining banks. As President Bush left office in 2009, the nation was experiencing the most severe economic recession since the Great Depression.

After his time in office, the Bushes returned to their ranch in Crawford, Texas, and also bought a home in Dallas. George took up painting and published a memoir of his time as president and a biography of his father, George H. W. Bush.

Name: _____ Date: _____

Recalling Key Details

Directions: Answer the following questions using what you have learned from the reading selection.

Matching:

____ 1. Office George W. Bush held before he was elected president   A. Texas governor

____ 2. Business Bush was involved in after he graduated from   B. Texas Rangers
       Harvard   C. pilot

____ 3. State where there was a controversy over the electoral   D. oil
       votes in the election of 2000   E. Florida

____ 4. Bush's job in the Texas Air National Guard

____ 5. Baseball team where Bush was the managing partner

Multiple Choice:

6. What locations were attacked by terrorists on September 11, 2001?
   A. The White House   B. The Washington Monument
   C. The World Trade Center   D. The Pentagon

7. Osama bin Laden and his al-Qaeda organization were protected by the Taliban, which ruled what country?
   A. Iraq   B. Afghanistan
   C. Iran   D. Syria

8. Which leader was captured, tried, and executed by the Iraqis?
   A. Osama bin Laden   B. Dick Cheney
   C. Saddam Hussein   D. George W. Bush

Structured Response:

9. Why did American troops remain in Afghanistan and Iraq after the old governments were toppled?

_____

_____

_____

10. What measures did the Bush administration take to try to restore the economy in 2008?

_____

_____

_____

_____

BARACK H. OBAMA
(1961–   , P. 2009–2017)

Barack Obama was born in Honolulu, Hawaii, on August 4, 1961, to a white mother from Kansas and a black father from Kenya. His parents divorced when he was four, and his mother married an Indonesian student. From 1967 to 1971, Obama lived with his family in Indonesia. In 1971, he returned to Hawaii and lived with his maternal grandparents until he went to college.

Obama graduated from Columbia University in 1983 and from Harvard Law School in 1988. After graduation, he taught constitutional law at the University of Chicago Law School. He met Michelle Robinson in 1989 at a Chicago law firm, and they married in 1991. They have two daughters, Malia and Sasha.

In 1996, Obama was elected to the Illinois State Senate and served there until 2004. He ran unsuccessfully for the U.S. House of Representatives in 2000, and then ran for U.S. Senate in 2004. Obama's keynote address at the 2004 Democratic National Convention in July brought him national attention. He easily won the senate seat in November and was talked about as a future contender for the office of president.

The election of 2008. Although Senator Hillary Clinton, wife of former President Bill Clinton, was the early Democratic frontrunner, Barack Obama unified the party with a message of hope and change. For the first time, an African American was a major-party candidate for president. Joe Biden, a long-time senator from Delaware, was the Democratic vice-presidential candidate. The Republicans endorsed Senator John McCain as their candidate. He was a decorated Vietnam veteran and prisoner of war and a popular, experienced senator from Arizona. He chose Sarah Palin, the governor of Alaska, as his running mate. During the campaign, both candidates returned to Washington, D.C., for votes in the Senate on financial relief measures to try to lift the economic recession. On Election Day, voters elected Barack Obama president. He won 52.9% of the popular vote and got 365 electoral votes to McCain's 173.

OBAMA AS PRESIDENT (first term). Obama was the first African American elected president. He chose his former opponent in the Democratic primary campaign, Hillary Clinton, to head the State Department.

President Obama began work by issuing executive orders directing the U.S. military to draw up plans for withdrawing troops from Iraq. He also ordered the closing of the detention camp that held suspected terrorists at Guantanamo Bay in Cuba, an action that was never fully carried out. Obama signed a bill making it easier for workers to file employment discrimination lawsuits. In March, he lifted the ban on federal tax dollars being used to fund embryonic stem cell research.

The American Recovery and Reinvestment Act was signed on February 17, 2009, a $787 billion spending bill to help the economy recover from the worldwide recession. The federal government also put billions of taxpayer dollars into the automotive industry in a takeover of Chrysler and General Motors as those companies went through bankruptcy.

Early in his term, Obama made a lasting impression on the judicial branch of government by appointing Sonia Sotomayor as an associate justice of the Supreme Court. Sotomayor was confirmed by the Senate on August 6, 2009. She was the first Hispanic to be a Supreme Court justice. He also appointed Elena Kagan to the Court, and she was confirmed in 2010.

Health care reform debate began in July 2009. Despite little support from Republicans, the House and Senate passed a health care reform bill and President Obama signed it in March 2010. The Affordable Care Act, also called "Obamacare" by critics, expanded insurance coverage and medical care to millions of Americans. However, the provision that all citizens must purchase health insurance or pay a tax was challenged in the Supreme Court. In 2012, the Court ruled it was allowed under Congress' taxation power. Many Americans actually lost their health insurance because of rising prices and the refusal of insurance companies to offer insurance in certain states. Republicans spent the rest of the Obama presidency trying to repeal the Affordable Care Act.

President Obama was awarded the 2009 Nobel Peace Prize, but many of his critics said he had not accomplished enough to deserve the award. Obama accepted the award as a call to action to promote peace.

Combat operations in Iraq ended by August 31, 2010, but a small number of U.S. military forces were kept in Iraq to support the Iraqi military and police. As insurgent attacks increased in Afghanistan and the Taliban regained strength, soldiers were shifted from Iraq to Afghanistan. Thousands more troops were sent to Afghanistan throughout 2010, but U.S. military involvement was scheduled to be reduced by July 2011.

One of the most dramatic events of Obama's presidency was the killing of the fugitive terrorist Osama bin Laden by Navy SEALs on May 2, 2011, in a compound in Abbottabad, Pakistan.

The election of 2012. Barack Obama and Joe Biden faced the Republican challengers Mitt Romney, former governor of Massachusetts, and his running mate, U.S. Representative from Wisconsin Paul Ryan. Several other minor-party candidates were also in the race. Obama and Romney raised a combined total of $2 billion in campaign funds, most of it spent on negative ads. Obama beat Romney 51 to 47 percent in the popular vote and 332 to 206 in electoral votes.

OBAMA AS PRESIDENT (second term). In 2013, Obama condemned Syria's leader Bashar al-Assad when he authorized the use of chemical weapons against Syrian civilians. In August 2014, after the extremist Islamic militant group called the Islamic State (ISIS or ISIL) had seized large areas of Syria and Iraq, killed thousands, and beheaded foreign hostages, Obama ordered air strikes against ISIS fighters. A global coalition was organized to fight ISIS.

Strides were made toward diplomacy in other areas. Obama reestablished diplomatic relations with Cuba and entered into an agreement with Iran concerning its nuclear program.

There were controversies over the National Security Agency's spying on citizens, the Internal Revenue Service's targeting of conservative political organizations, and accusations of a cover-up of the circumstances of the terrorist attack on the U.S. consulate in Benghazi, Libya, in September 2012. The attack resulted in the deaths of U.S. Ambassador Christopher Stevens and three others. Obama's approval rating was down to 37 percent by November 2013. In the November 2014 elections, the Republicans gained control of the Senate and kept their majority in the House. Obama's choice of Merrick Garland for the Supreme Court in March 2016 was blocked by the Republican leadership in the Senate. They claimed it was too close to the 2016 presidential elections, and the next president should be the one to fill the vacancy on the Court.

In order to deal with the effects of climate change and greenhouse gases, President Obama announced The Clean Power Plan, and the United States agreed to participate in the Paris Climate Agreement in 2015.

After Obama's time in office, the family moved to a Washington, D.C., neighborhood to allow daughter Sasha to continue at her school. They also maintained a residence in Chicago. Obama is working on writing a memoir of his time in politics, and he and Michelle have signed a deal with Netflix to create streaming content through their production company.

Name: _____ Date: _____

Recalling Key Details

Directions: Answer the following questions using what you have learned from the reading selection.

Matching:

____ 1. Title Barack Obama, John McCain, and Hillary Clinton
          shared during the 2008 presidential campaign

____ 2. Where Obama met his wife Michelle and taught
          constitutional law

____ 3. State where Obama was born

____ 4. What gained Obama national attention in 2004

____ 5. The American Recovery and Reinvestment Act was passed
          to help America recover from what?

A. keynote address

B. Hawaii

C. recession

D. Chicago

E. senator

Multiple Choice:

6. Which justices were appointed by Barack Obama to the Supreme Court and confirmed by the
    Senate?
    A. Elena Kagan   B. Ruth Bader Ginsburg
    C. Merrick Garland   D. Sonia Sotomayor

7. The Affordable Care Act expanded access to what?
    A. Clean energy   B. Taxpayer dollars for the automotive industry
    C. Stem cell research   D. Insurance coverage

8. Combat operations in Iraq ended, but where were more troops sent in 2010?
    A. Iran   B. Afghanistan
    C. Syria   D. Cuba

Structured Response:

9. What were some diplomatic actions that indicated Obama was working toward peace?

_____

_____

_____

10. Why was a global coalition formed to fight the Islamic State (ISIS)?

_____

_____

_____

DONALD J. TRUMP
(1946–   , P. 2017–   )

Donald John Trump was born on June 14, 1946, in Queens, New York. His father Frederick was a wealthy builder and real estate developer. Trump's mother Mary had immigrated from Scotland at the age of 17. She was involved in philanthropy and the New York social scene. Donald was the fourth of five children. He was sent to the New York Military Academy at age 13 and graduated in 1964. Trump attended Fordham University and then the Wharton School of Finance at the University of Pennsylvania, graduating in 1968 with a degree in economics. He did not serve in the Vietnam War due to education and medical deferments.

Like his father, Trump was a real estate developer. Many of his projects were large, highly visible developments in prime real estate areas, including Trump Tower in New York City and casinos in Atlantic City. Trump's businesses included The Trump Organization, Trump University, and selling a variety of merchandise. He wrote two books, including *The Art of the Deal*. Trump also became involved in producing and starring in reality television shows, such as the *Miss Universe* pageant and *The Apprentice*. Trump has been estimated to be worth over a billion dollars, but some of his business ventures have lost money over the years.

Trump has been married three times. He was married to his first wife, Ivana Zelnickova Winklmayr, a fashion model from Czechoslovakia, from 1977 to 1992. They had three children together: Donald Trump, Jr., Ivanka, and Eric. American actress Marla Maples was married to Trump from 1993 to 1999. Their daughter is named Tiffany. Trump married Melania Knauss, a model from Slovenia, in 2005. They have a teen-aged son named Barron. Donald Jr. and Eric now run The Trump Organization, and Ivanka and her husband Jared Kushner are advisers to the president.

Donald Trump switched political parties several times, with a brief run to get the presidential nomination of the Reform Party in 2000. He registered as a Democrat in 2001. He considered a run for president in 2012 as an Independent, but switched back to the Republican Party by the time of the 2012 election.

The election of 2016. A large field of candidates participated in the primary elections for both the Republicans and the Democrats. As the primary season wore on, Trump gained more support than the traditional politicians, and he won the Republican nomination, choosing Indiana Governor Mike Pence as his vice president. Hillary Rodham Clinton, former secretary of state, senator, and first lady, clinched the Democratic nomination. This was the first time a major party had chosen a female as their candidate. She chose Virginia Senator Tim Kaine as her running mate.

While Trump had no political experience, he appealed to conservative voters and campaigned hard in states like Michigan and Pennsylvania where voters felt left out of the economic recovery. Trump pledged to bring jobs back to America and to build a wall on the Mexican border, keeping illegal immigrants and drugs out. Despite not being "politically correct," his support grew, and Trump won the election in a surprise victory over Clinton by 304 to 227 in electoral votes. However, Clinton won the popular vote 48.3 to 46.2 percent. Almost immediately, protests broke out among liberal activists who did not agree with Trump or the results of the election.

TRUMP AS PRESIDENT. Trump worked quickly to carry out some of his campaign promises. Any criticism of his policies or negative information about his administration he dismissed as "fake news" from the "liberal media." Instead of press briefings, he often gave out his opinions and policy information on his social media account on Twitter.

In one of his first acts as president, Trump nominated Neil Gorsuch to the Supreme Court to fill the vacancy that had occurred during Barack Obama's last year in office. The conservative Gorsuch faced opposition from Democrats in the Senate, but the Republicans lowered the requirement to a simple majority to approve the nomination, and he was confirmed on April 7, 2017. Trump's nomination of Brett Kavanaugh for another vacancy on the Court met more opposition, as accusations of sexual assault were brought against Kavanaugh. However, after confirmation hearings and witness testimony, Kavanaugh was confirmed by a close vote in October 2018.

Through executive orders, Trump rolled back some of the policies of the Obama administration. He scaled back financial regulations, moved to repeal the Affordable Care Act, tightened travel restrictions to Cuba, and withdrew the U.S. from the Paris Climate Agreement. His budget proposed increased spending for the military, veterans, national security, and building a border wall. He wanted to cut funding for the EPA, the State Department, the arts, and social programs. He also withdrew from the Iran nuclear deal and reestablished sanctions against Iran.

Despite having a Republican majority in the House and Senate, efforts to repeal and replace the Affordable Care Act could not get enough support to pass. A tax reform bill was passed by the Senate in December 2017, which provided tax cuts for many and dropped the tax penalty for those who did not purchase medical insurance. Trump battled with Congress over spending bills that did not fully fund his programs, including a border wall with Mexico. There was a brief government shut-down in 2018 and a record 35-day shut-down in 2019. Congress and Trump eventually reached compromise deals, but in 2019, Trump declared a national emergency so he could use money earmarked for military construction for the border wall.

Trump is a supporter of Second Amendment gun rights, but after a number of horrific mass shootings, he has considered strengthening background checks and regulations on certain types of guns and accessories.

Allegations of Russian hacking to influence the 2016 election were verified by a report of the CIA, FBI, and NSA. An investigation by special counsel Robert Mueller could not find any evidence the Trump campaign had worked with the Russians, but did find other wrongdoing by Trump staffers.

Public outcry over separating the children of illegal immigrants from their families at the U.S. border and legal challenges to a travel ban on people from certain Muslim countries have hindered Trump's attempts to secure the nation's borders with these policies.

Using his skill as a businessman, President Trump negotiated a new trade deal with Canada and Mexico that was approved in 2019. New tariffs on certain foreign goods brought disapproval and retaliation from many nations around the globe. Trump specifically targeted China in order to get that country to make deals that were fairer to the United States. China and the United States went through a series of tariff hikes, but negotiations continued with China to come to a deal and avoid a trade war.

In December 2019, Trump established the U.S. Space Force to protect U.S. and allied interests in space and to provide capabilities for the U.S. military in space. The Pentagon is planning for this new branch of the military, which will be under the direction of the U.S. Air Force.

Foreign affairs. President Trump tried to establish better relations with North Korean dictator Kim Jong-un to lessen the tension between the two countries. Trump and Kim had two summit meetings in Singapore and Vietnam. Trump became the first U.S. president to visit North Korea while in office when he met with Kim at the Demilitarized Zone between North and South Korea on June 30, 2019. However, economic sanctions remain in place against North Korea to try to get them to dismantle their nuclear weapons program.

Air strikes on Syria continued in response to Syrian President Bashar al-Assad's use of chemical weapons on Syrian civilians. American and coalition forces were able to shrink the size of ISIS territory, and more troops were withdrawn from Syria and Iraq. In October 2019, an American commando raid in Syria killed the ISIS leader Abu Bakr Al-Baghdadi.

Iran sponsored protests against the American presence in Iraq. When an Iranian-backed militia launched a rocket attack on an Iraqi base, killing one American, the U.S. retaliated against that militia group. Protesters breached the outer wall of the U.S. embassy in Iraq. President Trump then ordered the U.S. military to carry out a drone strike near Baghdad, Iraq, on January 3, 2020, that killed Iran's top security and intelligence commander, General Qassem Soleimani. Trump said there was evidence that Soleimani was planning terrorist strikes against the United States. Iran retaliated by launching missiles at a U.S. air base in Iraq. No one was killed in the attack, but a Ukrainian passenger airliner taking off from Tehran was mistakenly shot down by an Iranian missile, killing all 176 on board. Both sides indicated they would refrain from further missile or drone attacks for the time being.

During the summer of 2019, President Trump had ordered military aid money to be withheld from Ukraine. He had then asked Ukrainian President Volodymyr Zelensky to investigate Hunter Biden's business activities in Ukraine to check for any corruption. Hunter is the son of Joe Biden, former vice president and one of the main Democratic candidates for president in the 2020 election. A whistleblower reported the phone call between Trump and Zelensky. Trump acknowledged the call with Zelensky, but he denied that he withheld the military aid in return for an investigation of Biden. This incident eventually led Speaker of the House Nancy Pelosi to announce they would begin an impeachment inquiry against Trump. After hearing from several witnesses, the House voted on December 18, 2019, in favor of two articles of impeachment: abuse of power (230 yes – 197 no) and obstruction of Congress (229 yes – 198 no). The vote was mostly along party lines with no Republicans voting to impeach. As of this printing, the Senate is beginning the trial to decide if President Trump will be removed from office. Chief Justice of the Supreme Court John Roberts will preside over the trial and the senators will act as the jury. Senate Majority Leader Mitch McConnell has said they will not call any witnesses. Since the Republicans hold a majority in the Senate (53 Republicans, 45 Democrats, 2 Independents), it is expected that Trump will be acquitted of the charges and remain in office.

Name: _____ Date: _____

Recalling Key Details

Directions: Answer the following questions using what you have learned from the reading selection.

Matching:

____ 1. Party in which Donald Trump ran for president briefly in 2000   A. border wall

____ 2. Trump's solution for keeping illegal drugs and immigrants   B. executive orders
out of the United States   C. Reform Party

____ 3. Where President Trump gives out most information to the   D. tariffs
public   E. Twitter

____ 4. What Trump used to roll back some of the Obama policies

____ 5. What Trump used to try to get China to negotiate fairer
trade deals with the United States

Multiple Choice:

6. Who are the justices of the Supreme Court that Trump has been able to appoint?

    A. Brett Kavanaugh   B. John Roberts

    C. Neil Gorsuch   D. Sonia Sotomayor

7. Trump became the first president to visit which country while in office?

    A. Ukraine   B. North Korea

    C. South Korea   D. Iraq

8. Trump was impeached by the House of Representatives on what two articles?

    A. Bribery   B. Abuse of power

    C. Obstruction of Congress   D. Collusion

Structured Response:

9. What were Congress and Trump battling over that led to a 35-day government shut-down?

_____

_____

_____

10. Why was the U.S. military ordered to kill Iranian General Qassem Soleimani with a drone
strike? How did Iran respond?

_____

_____

_____

_____

Enhancement Activities

Use these questions, prompts, and suggestions to complete discussion questions, graphic organizers, creative writing assignments, artistic projects, map analysis, and research opportunities about the presidents.

George Washington

1. Draw a picture or construct a model of a fort from the time of the French and Indian War.

2. Make a time line of Washington's military and political career.

3. Research Washington's home, Mount Vernon. Design a travel brochure, including pictures, describing both his home and the area. Convince people to visit.

4. Pretend you were a soldier serving under Washington. Describe his qualities as a good leader. Tell about some of the hardships you endured, especially in the winter.

John Adams

1. One of Adams' most important appointments was John Marshall, whom he named as Chief Justice. Why is the choice of justices on the Supreme Court important? Make a time line of John Marshall's career, or write a short biography of his life.

2. Adams called the vice presidency, "the most insignificant office that ever the invention of man contrived or his imagination conceived." What are the duties of the vice president? Make a chart or poster listing presidents that were formerly vice presidents. Include how they became president: through presidential assassination or death, resignation, impeachment, election.

Thomas Jefferson

1. Make a poster or write a journal as if you traveled with the Lewis and Clark Expedition. Include pictures and descriptions of the animals, plant life, and any Native Americans you saw along the way. What did you eat? What type of supplies did you take along?

2. Thomas Jefferson was accomplished in many areas of learning. Write a report on the many subjects he studied. How did this knowledge contribute to his success?

James Madison

1. Write a mini-report about the impressment of sailors and the *Chesapeake* Affair. Describe the connection to the War of 1812.

2. Write a short biography on Francis Scott Key or Dolley Madison. Include a picture. Share your knowledge with the class.

3. Make a poster of the Bill of Rights. Include a brief description of each amendment and what it means to you as an American.

James Monroe

1. Draw or construct a map of free and slave states at the time of the Missouri Compromise. Make the free states a different color from the slave states.

2. James Monroe was chosen as President Madison's secretary of state. Which other presidents served in this position?

3. Write a report on the history of Florida. How many countries claimed ownership throughout its history? During Monroe's presidency, why did the United States want it so badly?

John Quincy Adams

1. John Q. Adams traveled extensively as a young man, both as a student and as ambassador. Draw a map of his travels or write a journal about the sights he may have seen in Europe.

2. Following his term as president, John Q. Adams worked in the anti-slavery cause and for the better treatment of women. Stage a class debate on one of these topics.

3. Adams tried to treat the Creek people fairly, but Andrew Jackson treated Native Americans very cruelly. Write a mini-report on the Creek people and how they were treated during this period.

Andrew Jackson

1. Draw a map of the "Trail of Tears," or write a journal about the journey. Where did the Native Americans settle? What hardships along the way caused so many to perish?

2. "Remember the Alamo!" Pretend you are a reporter or an eyewitness during the Texas War for Independence. Report what you see, or interview Santa Anna or Sam Houston. Write a news article and include a picture.

Martin Van Buren

1. Van Buren "courted" the media. His manners and appearance helped his appeal. Pretend you are at a press conference. What questions would you ask him about the issues of his administration? How did the media in Van Buren's time compare to or differ from today?

2. The best-known abolitionist of Van Buren's time was William Lloyd Garrison, whose newspaper was the *Liberator*. Research the type of articles published in the *Liberator*, and then write an article promoting the abolitionist cause.

3. Write a short biography on Daniel Webster.

William Henry Harrison and John Tyler

1. Interview Tecumseh and his younger brother, Tenskwatawa, the Prophet. How did they differ in appearance and personality? Why was Tenskwatawa called "the Shawnee Prophet"? Which brother do you think was a better leader?

2. Write a newspaper article describing the campaign of 1840, the "hard cider" campaign. How was it different from those that had taken place before? Why was Harrison often portrayed as a simple farmer of humble birth and little education?

3. Henry Clay was never elected president; he did, however, actively participate in politics for many years. Make a time line of Henry Clay's political career.

James K. Polk

1. Make a map or time line of the annexation of states during this period.

2. Write a short biography on John C. Frémont or Winfield Scott.

3. If you opposed slavery, would you favor the Wilmot Proviso? Debate with members of your class on whether or not to support the Wilmot Proviso.

Zachary Taylor and Millard Fillmore

1. Make a model or drawing of the Washington Monument.

2. Write a newspaper article about the Gadsden Purchase and the building of the railroad.

3. Make a map of land given to the different Native American tribes at this time.

Franklin Pierce

1. Write a mini-report on camels in the United States.

2. Make a chart listing the major candidates of the Free Soil and Know-Nothing Parties.

James Buchanan

1. Read *Uncle Tom's Cabin* by Harriet Beecher Stowe. Give a book report on it.

2. As a class, research the Underground Railroad. Was there a stop on the Underground Railroad in your town or in a town near you? Have a class discussion on the outcome of your research.

Abraham Lincoln

1. Stage a mock debate about slavery, such as Lincoln and Douglas may have had.

2. Draw a sketch of an ironclad ship from the time of the Civil War or the submarine, the *Hunley*.

3. Make a map or make a time line of the battles won and lost by the North and South.

4. Have each member of the class select a famous person who was active during the Civil War and portray him or her in front of the class. Some suggestions are Sojourner Truth, Harriet Tubman, Stephen Foster, Mathew Brady, or General George McClellan.

Andrew Johnson

1. What were some of the laws for newly freed people that came to be known as the Black Codes? Make a chart or poster that illustrates some of the things that free African Americans were not allowed to do.

2. Discuss the carpetbaggers, their effect on Reconstruction, and their work with emancipated slaves.

3. Write a mini-report on the history of Alaska. Include who sold it to the United States and how much was paid for it.

Ulysses S. Grant

1. Using a blank map of the United States, draw the routes of the Union Pacific and the Central Pacific Railroads. Label the starting points of each railroad and the place where they met.

2. Make a graphic organizer of presidents who have been generals in war time. List the presidents, their ranks, and the war(s) they fought in.

Rutherford B. Hayes

1. Compare and discuss the Hayes/Tilden election with the election of 2000 between Al Gore and George W. Bush.

James Garfield, Chester Arthur, and Grover Cleveland

1. Compare the "Stalwarts" and "Half-Breeds." How did the split between Stalwarts and Half-Breeds affect Garfield's administration? How did the struggle between them affect the choice of Arthur for vice president? Discuss the corrupt political machines of Roscoe Conkling and Boss Tweed.

2. Pretend you are interviewing President Arthur regarding the Pendleton Civil Service Act. How did it affect the spoils system?

3. Write a short biography on John Philip Sousa. What songs and marches made him famous? Try to find recordings of some of his marches and play them for the class.

4. Draw a picture or make a diorama of a Pullman train car, or pretend you are interviewing President Cleveland or Eugene Debs and write a newspaper article about the American Railway Union strike.

Benjamin Harrison

1. Write a short biography on Thomas "Czar" Reed.

2. John Sherman was the younger brother of General William T. Sherman. Make a time line of his career or write a report on the Sherman Antitrust Act and the Silver Purchase Act.

William McKinley

1. Write a short biography about William Jennings Bryan and discuss his "Cross of Gold" speech, or write a report on the life of a coal miner during McKinley's presidency and the coal miners' strike.

2. Draw a map of the battles of the Spanish-American War.

Theodore Roosevelt

1. Find the Panama Canal on a map and discuss the turbulent history of the construction and control of the Canal. Make a time line.

2. In 1882, Teddy Roosevelt published his first book, *The Naval War of 1812*. Name some other presidents who have had literary works published. Discuss some of their works.

William Howard Taft

1. Write a report about Gifford Pinchot and his involvement with conservation and forestry. How do you think his ideas were similar to that of conservationists today?

2. Write a short biography about Joseph "Uncle Joe" Cannon.

Woodrow Wilson

1. Make a diorama or a poster about things Americans on the home front did to help the war effort, such as liberty bonds and gardens, the collection of scrap metal, and so on. Find copies of some advertising of the time that promoted the war effort.

2. Imagine that you were related to someone who died on the *Lusitania*. Compose an editorial to your newspaper or write a letter to President Wilson, expressing your feelings regarding the incident.

Warren Harding

1. Write a mini-report on the Teapot Dome Scandal and Secretary of the Interior Albert Fall.

2. Design a travel brochure for tourists, listing some places of interest in the United States, such as Mount Rushmore or Hoover Dam. Include a brief history and pictures of each place you choose.

Calvin Coolidge

1. Make a poster to show the growing businesses that were changing America during the Coolidge administration.

2. Write an interview with J. Edgar Hoover about his crackdown on the illegal manufacture and sale of alcohol.

Herbert Hoover

1. Interview someone who lived through the Great Depression. What are some of the things we take for granted that weren't available during that time? Share your findings with the class.

2. Write a report on the Boxer Rebellion in China. How was Hoover involved?

Franklin D. Roosevelt

1. Research polio. Write a report about the symptoms, treatment, and the polio vaccine.

2. Make a poster or chart about the New Deal. List the programs, such as the SEC, FDIC, AAA, REA, and so on. What were their purposes and benefits to Americans?

3. Stage a "Fireside Chat" such as FDR broadcast to the people of America. Why did these chats mean so much to Americans?

Harry S Truman

1. Discuss the outcome of the election of 1948. How did the published results differ from the true outcome? Why was Truman's victory in 1948 so surprising? Stage a class debate about the influence and power of the media in today's world. Does the media sometimes go too far in its reporting of events?

2. Research the life and career of one of the following: General Douglas MacArthur, Winston Churchill, or Joseph Stalin. Write a short biography or make a time line about the life of one of these famous men, and include a picture of him.

Dwight Eisenhower

1. Give an eyewitness account as if you were a member of the National Guard troops ordered by the governor of Arkansas to keep African-American students out of Little Rock Central High School. How did you feel about it?

2. Some Americans built bomb shelters during the 1950s. Write a mini-report. Discuss why they built them and what types of supplies they may have stored there. Do you know anyone who built a bomb shelter?

John F. Kennedy

1. Part of Kennedy's inaugural address, "and so, my fellow Americans..." is often quoted. List other famous quotations by former presidents.

2. Find or draw a picture of a patrol torpedo boat such as Kennedy's PT-109.

Lyndon B. Johnson

1. Research NASA and the Apollo Space Program. Write a report, build a model, or make a drawing of an Apollo spacecraft.

2. Conduct an interview or a debate regarding civil rights with Martin Luther King, Jr.; J. Edgar Hoover; or Malcolm X.

Richard Nixon

1. How many different presidents were involved in sending troops to Vietnam? Make a time line.

2. Interview someone who was a "witness" to Watergate. Write an article.

Gerald Ford

1. Write a short biography about Henry Kissinger.

2. Make a chart or poster listing which presidents were lawyers.

Jimmy Carter

1. Make a chart on different types of energy and ways to conserve it.

2. Research the boycotted Moscow Olympic Games of 1980: some athletes lost their chance to compete for an Olympic medal; some came back to compete in the next Olympics.

3. Write a report on the Ayatollah Khomeini and his hostages. How do released hostages cope with their freedom after their ordeal is over?

Ronald Reagan

1. Draw a map of the different areas of unrest around the world during the Carter and Reagan administrations.

2. Write a short biography on Geraldine Ferraro, the first woman vice-presidential candidate of a major political party.

George H. W. Bush

1. George H. W. Bush received a Distinguished Flying Cross for heroism during World War II. Draw a picture of this. Research to find other people who have been awarded this honor. How does the government decide who receives the Distinguished Flying Cross?

2. Draw or cut out pictures and make a poster about the oil spill of the *Exxon Valdez* and its effect on wildlife, both on land and in the ocean.

3. Draw a map of the Soviet Union. Compare the Soviet Union before and after its breakup.

William (Bill) Clinton

1. Try to find some cigarette ads from the past that promoted smoking. How has the public's awareness of smoking changed? What was the Food and Drug Administration's involvement? How did all this affect the tobacco companies?

2. Write a short report on the Brady Bill or AmeriCorps.

George W. Bush

1. George W. Bush's vice president, Dick Cheney, was the secretary of defense under former President George H. W. Bush and played a major part in Operation Desert Storm. Write a mini-report comparing Operation Desert Storm to the second invasion of Iraq known as Operation Iraqi Freedom.

2. Condoleezza Rice was an important member of the Bush administration. During George W. Bush's first term, Rice was the National Security Advisor. During Bush's second term, she was appointed secretary of state when Colin Powell stepped down. Research Condoleezza Rice's life and write a short biography.

Barack H. Obama

1. In order to become less involved in the Middle East, it is recommended that America become less dependent on foreign oil. List some of the ways Americans could use less foreign oil. What are some alternative fuels being developed?

2. Make a graphic organizer of the presidents who have received the Nobel Peace Prize and why they received that honor.

Donald J. Trump

1. Make a comparison of how presidents have used different types of media to get their message to the people throughout the years: newspapers, radio, television, websites, and social media. Write a short report giving examples for each type of media.

2. Research to see if you can find out how much money each president was worth when they were in office. Make a chart to show your findings.

Answer Keys

GEORGE WASHINGTON (p. 5)
1. F   2. T   3. F   4. T   5. F
6. D   7. C
8. Answers will vary.
9. They are able to take charge and make things happen, they are decisive, and are able to organize and develop a strategy.
10. They are used to giving orders, so they might not work well with others.

JOHN ADAMS (p. 7)
1. B   2. D   3. E   4. A   5. C
6. D   7. B   8. B, C
9. He lost Republican support over the Sedition Act, and then he lost Federalist support when he negotiated with France.
10. Preside over the Senate and vote in case of a tie; take over as president if something happens to the president

THOMAS JEFFERSON (p. 10)
1. D   2. B   3. A   4. E   5. C
6. C   7. B   8. D
9. The Court claimed the right to declare an act of Congress unconstitutional.
10. Answers will vary.

JAMES MADISON (p. 12)
1. C   2. A   3. E   4. B   5. D
6. B   7. A, C, D   8. A
9. She was a colorful, lively hostess. The Madison home became a center of social activity.
10. He participated in debates and worked on the compromises. He was one of the authors of the *Federalist Papers*, which explained the Constitution to the people. He promised a Bill of Rights after the Constitution was ratified.

JAMES MONROE (p. 14)
1. D   2. C   3. E   4. B   5. A
6. D   7. A   8. B
9. There was only one political party with any power, the Democratic-Republicans. Monroe easily won the presidency after Madison, and his reelection was even easier.
10. It allowed Missouri to enter the Union as a slave state and Maine to enter as a free state. Slavery would be forbidden in the Louisiana Purchase territories north of 36°30′N latitude.

JOHN QUINCY ADAMS (p. 16)
1. F   2. F   3. O   4. O   5 O
6. D   7. A, B, D   8. B
9. Henry Clay gave his support to Adams, which led to Adams' election. Then Adams appointed Clay as his secretary of state.
10. He had traveled to many countries (Holland, Portugal, Prussia, Sweden, Great Britain, Russia) and knew how to deal with world leaders.

ANDREW JACKSON (p. 19)
1. B   2. D   3. E   4. A   5. C
6. C   7. A   8. D
9. Rachel Jackson died and Jackson blamed it on Adams and Clay because they had brought out the accusations of bigamy.
10. The federal power would decrease because the government would be unable to make any state follow a law they didn't like.

MARTIN VAN BUREN (p. 21)
1. F   2. T   3. F   4. F   5. T
6. B   7. B, C   8. C
9. He focused on the welfare of the government, not the individuals who were suffering.
10. His family owned enslaved workers. He said Congress should not interfere with slavery because he feared the issue would split North and South. By 1844, he supported the anti-slavery movement and opposed annexing Texas as a slave state.

WILLIAM HENRY HARRISON (p. 23)
1. E   2. D   3. B   4. A   5. C
6. D   7. A   8. B
9. He thought that since the practice was legal, Indiana citizens should have the right to own slaves.
10. The campaign featured songs, jingles, parades, and barbecues. They emphasized Harrison's log cabin and hard cider background while claiming Van Buren was used to riches and French wine.

JOHN TYLER (p. 25)
1. A   2. C   3. D   4. B   5. E
6. C   7. D   8. B
9. Since they hadn't elected him to be president, they had a hard time following his orders or going along with his plans. They were just waiting for the next election so they could choose another president.
10. Since he had been elected to the Confederate House of Representatives during the Civil War, the U.S. government made no official announcement of his death.

JAMES K. POLK (p. 27)
1. B   2. D   3. A   4. C   5. E
6. D   7. B   8. C
9. They could have passed the Wilmot Proviso, which would have prevented the spread of slavery into the territory won in the war with Mexico.
10. He got the tariff reduced, created the Independent Treasury, set the Oregon border at 49°N latitude. He also expanded U.S. territory in the west to the Pacific Ocean by pushing the war with Mexico. This settled the Texas border and gained territory, including California.

ZACHARY TAYLOR (p. 29)
1. F   2. F   3. O   4. O   5. F
6. D   7. C   8. B
9. They admire the take-charge attitude and the ability to win victories in difficult situations.
10. The Southern states were threatening to secede from the Union if slavery couldn't be expanded into the territories. A compromise had to be found to keep the Union together.

MILLARD FILLMORE (p. 31)
1. E   2. D   3. A   4. B   5. C
6. D   7. C   8. A
9. The government let settlers move into the region.
10. The Compromise of 1850 was passed. Railroad construction grew and the Gadsden Purchase was made. Commodore Matthew Perry began diplomatic relations with Japan.

FRANKLIN PIERCE (p. 33)
1. B   2. C   3. A   4. E   5. D
6. C   7. D   8. A
9. Pierce thought that since the Constitution allowed slavery, it should be allowed in all states, no matter where they were located.
10. Pierce's father had been a Revolutionary War general and governor. Franklin had a fine record as a lawyer, state legislator, and in the U.S. House and Senate. He was well liked and charming.

JAMES BUCHANAN (p. 35)
1. E   2. D   3. A   4. C   5. B
6. B   7. C   8. A
9. Northern Democrats—Stephen Douglas
Southern Democrats—John C. Breckinridge
Republicans—Abraham Lincoln
Constitutional Union—John Bell
Abraham Lincoln won.
10. Buchanan did not feel he had the power to make them stay, possibly because his term was ending soon.

ABRAHAM LINCOLN (p. 38)
1. B   2. D   3. E   4. A   5. C
6. B   7. A   8. C
9. Lincoln could get more cooperation from foreign nations if he ended slavery. Black troops could serve in the Union army. Many Northerners now wanted slavery to end. Enslaved people might abandon the South if there was hope they could be free.
10. Lincoln was shot while attending Ford's Theatre. John Wilkes Booth, an actor and supporter of the Southern cause, shot Lincoln.

ANDREW JOHNSON (p. 40)
1. D   2. E   3. B   4. A   5. C
6. D   7 B   8. C
9. He hoped it would draw Democratic support and border staters to the ticket.
10. The Reconstruction of the South—pardoning Southerners, restoring government in the South, and granting rights to the formerly enslaved people

ULYSSES S. GRANT (p. 42)
1. B   2. A   3. D   4. E   5. C
6. A   7. C   8. B
9. He let Congress lead in making laws. He appointed friends to high positions, and he didn't realize they were corrupt.
10. To provide an income for his wife after he died

RUTHERFORD B. HAYES (p. 44)
1. D   2. C   3. B   4. A   5. E
6. D   7. C   8. A
9. Because the Grant administration had been known for corruption
10. Tilden had 184 electoral votes, Hayes had 165, and there were 20 disputed votes. The Electoral Commission ended up having 8 Republicans and 7 Democrats, so they voted along party lines, giving the electoral votes to Hayes.

JAMES GARFIELD (p. 46)
1. F   2. T   3. T   4. F   5. F
6. C   7. A   8. D
9. He was not going to be dictated to by senators when he made his appointments.
10. The assassin was a disappointed office seeker who supported the Stalwart branch of the party.

CHESTER ARTHUR (p. 48)
1. D   2. C   3. A   4. E   5. B
6. B   7. A   8. B
9. The assassin had been a disappointed office seeker. They wanted a fair way for government jobs to be filled.
10. Mail service was improved, the price of stamps dropped, Congress appropriated money for new steel ships, and major improvements were made to the White House.

GROVER CLEVELAND (p. 51)
1. C   2. D   3. E   4. B   5. A
6. C   7. D   8. C
9. Veterans, northern Industrialists, western ranchers and lumber companies, and labor unions turned against Cleveland because of his policies.
10. As railroad construction slowed, less steel and coal were needed, factories laid off workers. The unemployed and even those who had money stopped spending on goods and services.

BENJAMIN HARRISON (p. 53)
1. D   2. C   3. A   4. E   5. B
6. D   7. C   8. D
9. Harrison campaigned from his front porch, and Cleveland did not campaign and would not let his cabinet members campaign for him.
10. Congress was spending $989 million, and the public didn't think it was necessary.

WILLIAM McKINLEY (p. 55)
1. F   2. F   3. O   4. O   5. F
6. A   7. D   8. B
9. He was part of a group of volunteers called the Rough Riders who served in Cuba. He led the charge up San Juan Hill.
10. He was shot by an anarchist, Leon Czolgosz, on September 6, 1901, while in Buffalo, New York. He died on September 14.

THEODORE ROOSEVELT (p. 58)
1. D   2. E   3. A   4. B   5. C
6. B   7. A   8. D
9. When the people of Panama revolted against Colombia, Roosevelt quickly recognized Panama's independence. The U.S. then signed a treaty with Panama for a canal zone.
10. He set aside forest lands for national use, he enforced the Sherman Antitrust Act, and signed the Pure Food and Drug Act.

WILLIAM HOWARD TAFT (p. 60)
1. D   2. E   3. C   4. A   5. B
6. A   7. C   8. D
9. He could not get political or public support for his policies. Speaker of the House Joe Cannon stopped bills from being considered, but Taft failed to support an effort to take away some of Cannon's power. He lost Roosevelt's support and angered the wealthy Republican Party members.
10. It split the Republican vote so Wilson won the election.

WOODROW WILSON (p. 63)
1. A   2. D   3. E   4. B   5. C
6. C   7. B   8. D
9. They were forced to sign or face Allied armies invading their country.
10. Nations involved in the League could have tried to talk to solve their problems instead of going to war.

WARREN HARDING (p. 65)
1. C   2. B   3. A   4. E   5. D
6. B   7. C   8. A
9. Harry Daugherty, attorney general, took bribes. Charles Forbes of the Veterans Bureau sold sheets and towels from the veterans' hospitals. Albert Fall, secretary of the interior, arranged the sale of oil from government reserves.
10. He voted the way he thought the people back home wanted and was kind to business while in the U.S. Senate. As president, he let those he appointed do their jobs, and he didn't interfere.

CALVIN COOLIDGE (p. 67)
1. D   2. B   3. A   4. E   5. C
6. A   7. B, D   8. C
9. He felt "the business of America is business" and didn't want to do anything to slow the business growth of the 1920s.
10. Answers will vary. He may have felt he could learn more by listening. If he said very little, opponents couldn't use it against him. He was also shy.

HERBERT HOOVER (p. 69)
1. F   2. O   3. O   4. F   5. O
6. D   7. B   8. C
9. He encouraged business leaders, urging them to increase production and hire more workers, talked to states about new building projects, cut federal taxes, urged farmers to cut crop production, and tried lending money to banks, railroads, and other large businesses through the Reconstruction Finance Corporation.
10. You would be receiving even less money and would not be able to pay the bills and loans.

FRANKLIN D. ROOSEVELT (p. 73)
1. D 2. B 3. E 4. A 5. C
6. B 7. C 8. A
9. Eleanor kept FDR involved in politics and his law career after he was stricken with polio. She could meet world leaders and common people and make them feel welcome. She traveled to military bases and sent reports to FDR.
10. By 1940, there was a threat of war so voters didn't want to change leadership. In 1944, the United States was in the middle of World War II so they really didn't want to change leaders.

HARRY S TRUMAN (p. 76)
1. D 2. C 3. A 4. B 5. E
6. B 7. D 8. B
9. Truman ordered striking coal miners and railway workers to go back to work. He threatened to draft the railway workers. The coal miners' union was fined $3.5 million. He vetoed the Taft-Hartley Labor Law.
10. The United States would support free people to resist Communism. It provided aid to Greece and Turkey.

DWIGHT EISENHOWER (p. 79)
1. E 2. C 3. D 4. A 5. B
6. D 7. A 8. C
9. In 1954, in *Brown v. Board of Education*, the Court said segregation in education violated the 14th Amendment. The Court also ruled segregation on buses was illegal.
10. Each department head was responsible for their own department. They were blamed instead of Eisenhower.

JOHN F. KENNEDY (p. 82)
1. B 2. D 3. E 4. A 5. C
6. B, D 7. C 8. D
9. Kennedy sent Green Berets to train the South Vietnamese how to fight more effectively.
10. Kennedy sent troops to West Berlin to keep the Soviets from taking over. He set up a blockade around Cuba to keep the Soviets from placing missiles with nuclear weapons on the island.

LYNDON B. JOHNSON (p. 85)
1. T 2. F 3. F 4. T 5. F
6. A 7. C 8. D
9. People began to think the big government programs had gone too far. Race riots broke out. The war in Vietnam was unpopular. Johnson kept sending more troops. Young people demonstrated against the war and the draft.
10. The reasoning was that if the United States sent so much force, the North Vietnamese would be forced to make peace.

RICHARD NIXON (p. 88)
1. E 2. D 3. C 4. B 5. A
6. B 7. C 8. A
9. Nixon reduced the number of U.S. troops from 543,000 to 39,000 in 1972. He relied on bombing attacks on North Vietnam. Bombing attacks on Viet Cong supply lines through Laos and Cambodia also began.
10. A witness said conversations had been held in the president's office about covering up CREEP's role. A recording device had taped the conversations, and the Supreme Court ordered those tapes turned over to the special prosecutor.

GERALD FORD (p. 90)
1. E 2. C 3. A 4. B 5. D
6. C 7. B, D 8. A
9. To begin the national healing process after Watergate and to save Nixon and his family from further suffering
10. The governments of both countries fell to Communist forces in April 1975. Some Vietnamese children and adults and all remaining Americans were airlifted out of South Vietnam.

JIMMY CARTER (p. 93)
1. D 2. C 3. A 4. E 5. B
6. A, D 7. B 8. D
9. His greatest success was bringing Israeli Prime Minister Menachem Begin and Egyptian President Anwar al-Sadat to talks at Camp David, which resulted in the peace treaty signed in 1979.
10. He has been involved in many peace-keeping and humanitarian efforts. The Carter Center was established to advance human rights and alleviate human suffering. He and Rosalynn participate in Habitat for Humanity. He has been on peace-keeping missions to Haiti and North Korea. He has worked for fair elections in South America, Europe, Africa, and the Middle East. He won the Nobel Peace Prize in 2002.

RONALD REAGAN (p. 96)
1. C 2. A 3. B 4. E 5. D
6. A, C, D 7. B 8. D
9. The United States set up missiles in West Germany that could reach the Soviet Union. The Soviets built up their military power. Reagan pushed the Strategic Defense Initiative to put weapons in space.
10. The new Soviet Premier Mikhail Gorbachev began changes in the Soviet Union that led to democracy. Meetings were held in Switzerland and Iceland, and agreements were made to destroy many missiles on both sides.

GEORGE H. W. BUSH (p. 99)
1. C 2. A 3. E 4. B 5. D
6. B 7. C 8. D
9. Boris Yeltsin resigned from the Communist Party and was elected president of the Russian Soviet Socialist Republic. Mikhail Gorbachev resigned as president of the Soviet Union and the Union of Soviet Socialist Republics dissolved. The former republics could become independent nations or join the Commonwealth of Independent States.
10. Unemployment was high and people were worried about the economy. His popularity dropped fast.

WILLIAM (BILL) CLINTON (p. 102)
1. O 2. F 3. O 4. O 5. F
6. B 7. A 8. D
9. In February 1993, the North Tower of the World Trade Center was attacked by extremist Muslims with a truck bomb, killing six people. On October 12, 2000, the USS *Cole* was bombed by terrorists while docked in Yemen, killing 17 sailors.
10. When the economy was bad in 1992, Clinton used it against George H. W. Bush. When the economy was good in 1996, Clinton used it as a reason for voters to keep him in office.

GEORGE W. BUSH (p. 105)
1. A 2. D 3. E 4. C 5. B
6. C, D 7. B 8. C
9. To see that free elections could he held and to help set up the new governments
10. Tax refunds were given to lower- and middle-class families, more funding was provided for government-based mortgage lenders to help homeowners faced with foreclosure, and up to $700 billion was authorized to prop up the remaining banks.

BARACK H. OBAMA (p. 108)
1. E 2. D 3. B 4. A 5. C
6. A, D 7. D 8. B
9. Obama reestablished diplomatic relations with Cuba and entered into an agreement with Iran concerning its nuclear program.
10. The extremist Islamic militant group had seized large areas of Syria and Iraq, killed thousands, and beheaded foreign hostages.

DONALD J. TRUMP (p. 112)
1. C 2. A 3. E 4. B 5. D
6. A, B 7. B 8. B, C
9. Spending bills that did not fully fund Trump's projects, including the border wall with Mexico
10. Iran had been sponsoring protests and militia rocket attacks against the U.S. forces in Iraq. There was evidence Soleimani was planning terrorist attacks against the United States. Iran fired missiles at a U.S. air base in Iraq. Iranian missiles accidentally hit a passenger plane, killing 176.

U.S. Presidents Photo Credits

pg. 3   Gilbert Stuart George Washington Phoenix Art Museum.jpg {PD-Old} Painting by Gilbert Stuart. c. 1796. Wmpearl. 12 Aug. 2019. <https://commons.wikimedia.org/wiki/File:Gilbert_Stuart_George_Washintong_Phoenix_Art_Museum.jpg>

pg. 6   John Adams, Gilbert Stuart, c1800 1815.jpg {PD-Old} Painting by Gilbert Stuart. c. 1800–1815. National Gallery. Werdna6102. 31 Oct. 2016. <https://commons.wikimedia.org/wiki/File:John_Adams,_Gilbert_Stuart,_c1800_1815.jpg>

pg. 8   Official Presidential portrait of Thomas Jefferson (by Rembrandt Peale, 1800).jpg {PD-Old} Painting by Rembrandt Peale. 1800. White House Collection. Futurist110. 8 Jul. 2012. <https://commons.wikimedia.org/wiki/File:Official_Presidential_portrait_of_Thomas_Jefferson_(by_Rembrandt_Peale,_1800).jpg>

pg. 11   James Madison.jpg {PD-Old} Painting by John Vanderlyn. 1816. White House Collection. Ibn Battuta. 9 March 2007. <https://commons.wikimedia.org/wiki/File:James_Madison.jpg>

pg. 13   Jamesmonroe-npgallery.jpg {PD-Old} Painting by John Vanderlyn. 1816. National Portrait Gallery. Les Meloures. 31 Dec. 2010. <https://commons.wikimedia.org/wiki/File:Jamesmonroe-npgallery.jpg>

pg. 15   JohnQAdams.png {PD-Old} Painting by George P. A. Healy. c. 1820s–1830s. Manchiu. 9 Feb. 2010. <https://commons.wikimedia.org/wiki/File:JohnQAdams.png>

pg. 17   Andrew jackson head.jpg {PD-Old} Painting by Ralph Eleaser Whiteside Earl. 1835. White House Collection. Magasjukur2. 17 Jan. 2011. <https://commons.wikimedia.org/wiki/File:Andrew_jackson_head.jpg>

pg. 20   Mvanburen.jpg {PD-Old} Painting by George P. A. Healy. 1858. White House Collection. Futurist110. 8 Jul 2012. <https://commons.wikimedia.org/wiki/File:Mvanburen.jpg>

pg. 22   William Henry Harrison by James Reid Lambdin, 1835.jpg {PD-Old} Painting by James Reid Lambdin. 1835. White House Collection. Scewing. 2 May 2010. <https://commons.wikimedia.org/wiki/File:William_Henry_Harrison_by_James_Reid_Lambdin,_1835.jpg>

pg. 24   Johntyler.jpg {PD-Old} Painting by George P. A. Healy. 1864. White House Collection. Igor Filippov. 20 Jun. 2005. <https://commons.wikimedia.org/wiki/File:Johntyler.jpg>

pg. 26   JamesKnoxPolk.jpg {PD-Old} Painting by George P. A. Healy. 1846. Catalog of American Portraits. Wow. 11 Oct. 2018. <https://commons.wikimedia.org/wiki/File:JamesKnoxPolk.jpg>

pg. 28   Zachary Taylor by Joseph Henry Bush, c1848.jpg {PD-Old} Painting by Joseph Henry Bush. c. 1848. White House Collection. Scewing. 2 May 2010. <https://commons.wikimedia.org/wiki/File:Zachary_Taylor_by_Joseph_Henry_Bush,_c1848.jpg>

pg. 30   Mfillmore.jpeg {PD-Old} Painting by George P. A. Healy. 1857. White House Collection. Futurist110. 8 Jul. 2010. <https://commons.wikimedia.org/wiki/File:Mfillmore.jpeg>

pg. 32   Franklin Pierce.jpg {PD-Old} Photograph by Mathew Brady. c. 1855-1865. Library of Congress. Grenavitar. 5 Apr. 2005. <https://commons.wikimedia.org/wiki/File:Franklin_Pierce.jpg>

pg. 34   James Buchanan, by George Peter Alexander Healy.jpg {PD-Old} Painting by George P. A. Healy. 1859. National Portrait Gallery. Gemicat16~commonswiki. 13 Nov. 2009. <https://commons.wikimedia.org/wiki/File:James_Buchanan,_by_George_Peter_Alexander_Healy.jpg>

pg. 36   Abraham Lincoln head on shoulders photo portrait.jpg {PD-Old} Photograph by Alexander Gardner. 8 Nov. 1863. Library of Congress. Tom. 4 Mar. 2006. <https://commons.wikimedia.org/wiki/File:Abraham_Lincoln_head_on_shoulders_photo_portrait.jpg>

pg. 39   Andrew johnson2.jpg {PD-Old} Photograph by Mathew Brady. 16 Jun. 1865. Library of Congress. ¡0-8-15! 6 Jun. 2005. <https://commons.wikimedia.org/wiki/File:Andrew_johnson2.jpg>

pg. 41   Ulysses S. Grant 1870-1880.jpg {PD-Old} Brady-Handy Photographic Collection. c. 1870–1880. Library of Congress.MarkSweep. 26 Dec. 2004. <https://commons.wikimedia.org/wiki/File:Ulysses_S._Grant_1870-1880.jpg>

pg. 43   President Rutherford Hayes 1870-1880.jpg {PD-Old} Photograph by Mathew Brady. c. 1870–1880. Library of Congress. Tom. 13 Jul. 2005. <https://commons.wikimedia.org/wiki/File:President_Rutherford_Hayes_1870-1880.jpg>

pg. 45   James Abram Garfield, photo portrait seated.jpg {PD-Old} Brady-Handy Photographic Collection. c. 1870–1880. Library of Congress. Tom. 4 Mar. 2006. <https://commons.wikimedia.org/wiki/File:James_Abram_Garfield,_photo_portrait_seated.jpg>

pg. 47   Chester Alan Arthur.jpg {PD-Old} Photograph by Charles Milton Bell. 1882. Library of Congress. ¡0-8-15! 6 Jun. 2005. <https://commons.wikimedia.org/wiki/File:Chester_Alan_Arthur.jpg>

pg. 49   [Grover Cleveland, bust portrait, seated, facing right] {PD-Old} c. 1880–1900. Library of Congress. <https://www.log.gov/item/2014648289/>